THE LAST DAYS OF BRITISH STEAM

A SNAPSHOT OF THE 1960s

THE LAST DAYS OF BRITISH STEAM

A SNAPSHOT OF THE 1960s

MALCOLM CLEGG

PEN & SWORD
TRANSPORT

AN IMPRINT OF PEN & SWORD BOOKS LTD.
YORKSHIRE – PHILADELPHIA

First published in Great Britain in 2020 by
Pen and Sword Transport
An imprint of
Pen & Sword Books Ltd
Yorkshire - Philadelphia

ISBN 978 1 52676 042 5

Typeset by Aura Technology and Software Services, India.
Printed and bound in India by Replika Press Pvt. Ltd.

Pen & Sword Books Ltd incorporates the Imprints of Pen & Sword Books Archaeology, Atlas, Aviation, Battleground, Discovery, Family History, History, Maritime, Military, Naval, Politics, Railways, Select, Transport, True Crime, Fiction, Frontline Books, Leo Cooper, Praetorian Press, Seaforth Publishing, Wharncliffe and White Owl.

For a complete list of Pen & Sword titles please contact

PEN & SWORD BOOKS LIMITED
47 Church Street, Barnsley, South Yorkshire, S70 2AS, England
E-mail: enquiries@pen-and-sword.co.uk
Website: www.pen-and-sword.co.uk

or

PEN AND SWORD BOOKS
1950 Lawrence Rd, Havertown, PA 19083, USA
E-mail: Uspen-and-sword@casematepublishers.com
Website: www.penandswordbooks.com

CONTENTS

INTRODUCTION

The 1960s were not the finest years in the history of Britain's railways, due to the effects of the Second World War and subsequent government transport policies.

By the end of the Second World War, the railways, which had been under government control during the war years, were in turmoil after six years of neglect, excessive use and virtually no maintenance. They were almost in a state of bankruptcy and in no fit state to be handed back to the 'Big Four' pre-war railway companies. Consequently, Britain's railways were nationalised on 1 January 1948.

After the war, most countries in Europe decided to change from steam to diesel or electric traction as a source of power on their railways. Britain decided upon a different course of action. Diesel was not an immediate option due to Britain not having any oil reserves. It would take several years before diesel traction could be introduced onto the railways.

Electrification was the preferred option and had been successfully used on parts of the Southern Railway before the outbreak of war. Electrification was, however, the most expensive option and prohibitive in the short term due to cost, although it would be gradually introduced over a long period of time, as and when finance was available.

It was therefore decided that 'steam' would continue as the main source of power for the foreseeable future. Steam locomotives were reliable and railway workshops were still well equipped to carry on building them. Although there was a coal shortage immediately after the war, coal in Britain was plentiful and still reasonably cheap and the coal mining industry was a valuable source of employment in need of support. Consequently, the building and introduction of new steam locomotives continued until 1960.

The first real signs that steam traction was to be abolished on Britain's railways was confirmed in 1955 when a new British Railways Modernisation Plan was introduced by the British government. The plan included a programme to introduce in excess of 4,500 diesel railcars onto the railway network. Consequently, from 1956 onwards, British Railways' 'First Generation' Diesel Multiple Units started to appear on the railways to replace steam-hauled passenger trains for local and branch line services.

1959 saw a Conservative government led by Harold Macmillan returned to power with a third consecutive election victory. He appointed Ernest Marples as the Minister of Transport. This appointment was to have far-reaching consequences for the railway industry. Mr Marples made no secret of the fact that he considered the railways to be an old-fashioned and outdated mode of transport. He believed that the future of transport lay not in the railways, but in the construction of a large network of new fast roads and extensive motorways throughout Britain.

He had personal interests in the oil industry, road lobby and the construction industry. He had owned 80 per cent of 'Marples-Ridgeway', a road construction company which had just completed building the M1 Motorway. He sold his shares to his wife when he became the Minister of Transport in order to avoid a 'conflict of interest' but had the option of buying them back when he left his ministerial office. In his capacity as Transport Minister, one of his first jobs was to formally open the M1 motorway which he did shortly after taking up office.

Ernest Marples also supported mass car production and he believed that cars should not only be available to the rich and famous, but should be affordable and widely available for middle and working class families. He himself owned a Mini Cooper S hatchback motor car which was specially built for him by the British Motor Corporation at Longbridge.

From 1960 onwards, the new government policy was set. Ernest Marples had been instrumental in persuading the government to invest in a new road network and extensive motorway construction. The government announced that Britain's future lay with road transport, as opposed to a loss-making outdated railway network built in the Victorian era.

The decision to officially replace steam locomotives with diesel was accelerated when it was decided that it was uneconomical to gradually introduce diesel locomotives to replace steam. This, it was said, would lead to a two-tier system of motive power (excluding electric) whereby both diesel and steam locomotives would be operating for many years on the same railway network. It was decided that the rapid withdrawal of all steam locomotives would take place and they would be replaced as quickly as possible by diesel locomotives. The hasty demise of steam locomotives took place during the 1960s. Thousands of locomotives were withdrawn almost overnight, destined for the scrapyards. Many of these were less than ten years old, with a life span of thirty to forty years; nevertheless, they were scrapped.

Vast numbers of railway coal wagons were also scrapped during the late 1950s and early 1960s as the demand for coal also declined, in part due to using diesel as opposed to coal to fuel the railway industry. Between 1960 and 1968, all British Railway steam locomotives, of which there were over thirteen thousand, were withdrawn from service. A few survived for preservation but the majority were scrapped.

A number of other changes took place on the railways during the 1960s, which were even more radical than the withdrawal of steam. In 1962, the 'British Transport Commission', the body responsible for running the railways, was abolished and replaced by the newly created 'British Railways Board'. Ernest Marples appointed Richard Beeching as Chairman and head of the new British Railways Board. Beeching, who had no previous railway experience whatsoever, was given the task of reducing the railway's huge deficit and cut spiralling losses. In 1963, he produced a report entitled 'The Reshaping of British Railways'.

The report, which later became known as 'The Beeching Report' or 'The Beeching Axe', concluded that much of the railway network was under-used and should be closed down. The report proposed a massive programme which would involve the closure of 2,363 railway stations and over 5,000 miles of track. Ernest Marples and the government backed the closures and most of them were implemented during the next few years.

By the end of the 1960s, Britain's railways had changed almost beyond recognition from those which had existed a decade earlier. During the 1950s, there were hundreds of small rural picturesque railway stations with their immaculate gardens and floral hanging baskets throughout Britain. The local Station Masters, who had been prominent figures in local communities since Victorian times, were ever present in their smart uniforms, adorned with gold braid embroidery, to ensure the efficient running of the railways and close supervision of staff. Station Masters often entered railway competitions for 'best kept stations' and 'best station gardens'. First, second and third 'prize certificates' were awarded in both categories to successful candidates who took great pride in receiving them.

As the railways entered the 1960s, the sweeping changes mentioned earlier were implemented. Large numbers of stations and branch lines began to close and the position of 'Station Master' was abolished. Villages became isolated and reliant on road transport as a means of communication. Strong protests were made by many residents in communities nationwide who attempted to save their railway lines and local stations from closure but only a small handful of these pressure groups had any success.

The photographs in this book were all taken in the 1960s during the hasty demise of steam. In the main, they do not depict the well maintained locomotives which operated during the 'golden days of steam' or the clean shiny locomotives which grace our heritage railways today. Instead, they reflect the last few years of steam locomotives operating on an underfunded railway network which was experiencing heavy financial losses, large scale closures, radical changes and an uncertain future. As can be seen from the photographs, many locomotives in service at the time were in a dirty and shabby condition, operating on what was in many places a run-down and dilapidated railway network.

Credits and Copyright

As is often the case with photographic collections, exchanges between collectors and the acquisition of other collections sometimes makes it impossible to credit the original photographer with a particular picture. There are also occasions when the same basic picture is taken by different photographers, especially on works and locomotive shed visits. For these reasons, the illustrations appearing in this book are simply credited to the 'Peter Cookson Collection' (marked PC), © Peter Cookson, or to the 'Author's Collection' (marked MC), © Malcolm Clegg.

Acknowledgement.

I would like to offer my sincere thanks and appreciation to Mr Peter Cookson for providing valuable assistance and allowing the publication of photographs from his private collection in this book.

LIST OF ABBREVIATIONS

Most frequently used abbreviations (Railway Companies).

BR = British Railways. **GWR** = Great Western Railway. **LMS** = London, Midland and Scottish (Railway). **LNER** = London and North Eastern Railway. **SR** = Southern Railway.

Other abbreviations.

CR = Caledonian Railway. **GCR** = Great Central Railway. **GNR** = Great Northern Railway. **IOW** = Isle of Wight (railway). **LYR** = Lancashire and Yorkshire Railway. **LBSCR** = London, Brighton and South Coast Railway. **LNWR** = London and North Western Railway. **LSWR** = London and South Western Railway. **MR** = Midland Railway. **NBR** = North British Railway. **NER** = North Eastern Railway. **SDR (SDJR)** = Somerset and Dorset (Joint) Railway. **SEC** = South East and Chatham Railway.

Types of tank locomotive.

T = Tank locomotive (ordinary).
PT = Pannier Tank locomotive.
ST = Saddle Tank locomotive.

Class of locomotive (Southern Railway locomotives).

BB = Battle of Britain Class. **LN** = Lord Nelson Class. **MN** = Merchant Navy Class. **WC** = West Country Class.

Locomotive Power Classification (BR System).

British Railways used a universal power classification for locomotives, derived from their pulling power and speed ratio. The system adopted by BR in 1948 was based on a slightly modified numbering system which had been used by the LMS (and Midland Railway), whereby the various types (classes) of locomotive were given a power classification number, ranging from zero to eight (**0-8**) for passenger locomotives and zero to nine (**0-9**) for freight locomotives.

Zero was regarded as the least powerful locomotive and nine was the most powerful. The number was painted on the side of the cab, together with a suffix, letter **'P'** or **'F'**, which denoted whether the locomotive was designed for passenger or freight work. For example; '**8P**' denoted the most powerful express passenger locomotives whilst '**9F**' was awarded to the most powerful class of freight locomotives (freight locomotives included shunting and banking engines). Locomotives classified as '**0F**' or '**1F**' would usually indicate a small shunting engine, whilst '**5P**' would be allocated to a standard passenger locomotive. '**3F**' would indicate a light freight / goods locomotive.

A locomotive designed for both passenger and freight work was known as a mixed traffic locomotive (**MT**). These locomotives either displayed two power classification numbers with the letter '**P**' rating first, followed by the '**F**' rating (example **6P5F**) or if the '**P**' and '**F**' ratings were the same they were given a single 'mixed traffic' (**MT**) rating (example **5MT**).

Other abbreviations.

WD = War Department. **ROD** = Railway Operating Division. Locomotives used for wartime service were under the control of the British Army, Royal Engineers, Railway Operating Division, or **ROD**.

IMAGES

A spectacular sight as this LNER 'Class A2/3' locomotive, number 60520 *Owen Tudor,* emits an abundance of grey/black smoke (likely caused by using poor quality coal) from her double chimney as she prepares to depart York Station with an express passenger train to King's Cross in 1960. *(Photo © PC).*

LNER. 'Class A3' locomotive, number 60066, *Merry Hampton,* pictured working a passenger express at York Station in 1960. A young boy standing on the opposite platform appears to be mesmerised by the locomotive. The city of York, with its long railway history, has been a magnet for train spotters and photographers for many years and is the home of the National Railway Museum. *(Photo © PC).*

LNER. 'Class A4' locomotive, number 60001, *Sir Ronald Matthews*, pictured at York Station in 1960 whilst working a Glasgow to King's Cross express passenger train via Edinburgh. This large, powerful pacific locomotive dwarfs an LNER 'Class J72' 0-6-0 Tank engine, number 68736, which is working as the station pilot engine, shunting passenger coaches alongside her. *(Photo © PC)*.

LNER. 'Class A2/2' locomotive, number 60504, *Mons Meg*, pictured in York Station in 1960. This was a rare sight in the 1960s as just six of these 'Class A2/2' locomotives were built, with the last member of the class (60502) being withdrawn the following year. Sadly, they were all scrapped. *(Photo © PC)*.

A dull, damp day at Swansea as this GWR 'Castle Class' locomotive, number 5060, *Earl of Berkeley*, prepares to leave Swansea High Street Station with an express passenger train to Paddington on 16 August 1960. 'Castle Class' locomotives usually worked the London services at the time. *(Photo © PC)*.

GWR 'Castle Class' locomotive number 4082, *Windsor Castle*, tender filled with coal but not in steam, was observed standing outside Swindon Works on 19 August 1963. 4082 was based at Gloucester Horton Road Shed at the time and continued working for another year before being withdrawn from service. She was cut up at Cashmores scrapyard, Newport, in January 1965. *(Photo © MC)*.

GWR 'King Class' locomotive, number 6018, *King Henry VI*, pictured speeding through Banbury with the 12.55pm Wolverhampton to Paddington express on 9 August 1962. *(Photo © PC)*.

Two GWR 'King Class' locomotives, number 6025, *King Henry III*, and number 6026, *King John*, pictured outside Swindon Works on 19 August 1963, having been withdrawn from service and waiting to be cut up for scrap. The nameplates, cab-side number plates and shed plates have all been removed from both engines, as have the tenders. *(Photo © MC)*.

SR. Rebuilt 'West Country Class' locomotive number 34031, *Torrington*, pictured working a busy Weymouth to Waterloo, Channel Island boat train through Upwey near Weymouth, Dorset, in August 1962. *(Photo © PC).*

SR. Un-rebuilt 'Battle of Britain Class' locomotive, number 34054, *Lord Beaverbrook*, entering Templecombe Station with a passenger express on 19 August 1963. The gentleman with the rucksack seen leaning against the fence appeared to be enthralled by the scene. *(Photo © MC).*

SR. 'Merchant Navy Class' locomotive, number 35019 *French Line CGT*, pictured letting off steam through her safety valve as she departs Bournemouth Central with an up express passenger train to Waterloo in August 1962. *(Photo © PC).*

SR. Rebuilt 'Battle of Britain Class' locomotive, number 34077, *603 Squadron*, pictured at Nine Elms Shed in South London together with 'WC Class' number 34104, *Bere Alston*, and 'Rebuilt MN Class' number 35024, *East Asiatic Company,* in 1964. *(Photo © PC).*

LMS, 'Jubilee Class' locomotive, number 45737, *Atlas*, pictured working an express passenger train service through Mirfield, West Yorkshire, in 1961. *(Photo © PC).*

LMS, 'Princess Royal Class' locomotive, number 46206, *Princess Marie Louise*, at Crewe Station, working an express passenger train to Liverpool on 2 August 1961. *(Photo © PC).*

LMS, 'Royal Scot Class' locomotive, number 46130, *The West Yorkshire Regiment*, pictured at Sheffield Midland Station, preparing to depart with an express passenger train to London, St. Pancras on 3 September 1960. *(Photo © PC)*.

A magnificent sight for a steam enthusiast but not for the modern day environmentalist as this LMS 'Patriot Class' locomotive number 45505, *The Royal Army Ordnance Corps*, works its way through Skipton, North Yorkshire, with an express passenger train on 24 April 1962, discharging clouds of smoke in its wake. *(Photo © PC)*.

LNER 'Class A1' locomotive, number 60147, *North Eastern*, has seen better days as she works an express freight train through Doncaster Station in 1964, a far cry from the work she was designed for. She was withdrawn from service in August 1964, just after this picture was taken. *(Photo © PC).*

BR. Standard 'Britannia Class' locomotive, number 70015, *Apollo,* pictured at the former Pontypool Road Station in June 1964 whilst working a Cardiff to Manchester express passenger service. *(Photo © MC).*

BR. Standard 'Clan Class' locomotive, number 72000, *Clan Buchanan*, pictured at Hest Bank, Morecambe, working a passenger express in 1961. It was not uncommon for poor quality coal to be used on locomotives in the 1950s and 1960s, often resulting in the discharge of excessive black smoke. This did however produce some spectacular images for photographers. *(Photo © PC).*

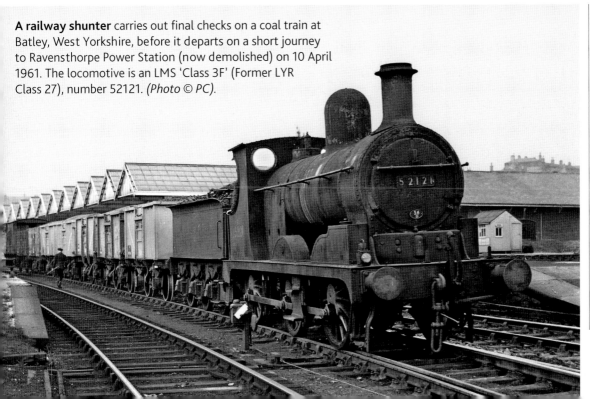

A railway shunter carries out final checks on a coal train at Batley, West Yorkshire, before it departs on a short journey to Ravensthorpe Power Station (now demolished) on 10 April 1961. The locomotive is an LMS 'Class 3F' (Former LYR Class 27), number 52121. *(Photo © PC).*

GWR '5700 Class' Pannier Tank locomotive, number 4623, pictured at Cardiff East Dock Shed on 18 April 1965. Both the smokebox number plate and shed plate are missing from the engine and the building behind the locomotive is in a shabby condition with several broken windows. *(Photo © MC).*

GWR 'Class 1400' Tank locomotive, number 1455, pictured at Gloucester Central Station waiting to depart with a local auto-train service to Chalford in the summer of 1964. The dilapidated locomotive is still displaying the early BR lion and wheel emblem (pre 1956) on her side tanks. A condemned passenger coach can be seen in the background. *(Photo © MC).*

SR (LSWR). **'Class** 0415' Adams Tank locomotive, number 30583. Pictured as a light engine at Lyme Regis in May 1960. This engine was sold to the WD during the First World War and later re-sold to the Southern Railway. After being withdrawn from service in July 1961, she was purchased by the Bluebell Heritage Railway where she is on static display awaiting an overhaul. *(Photo © PC)*.

SR (LSWR). **'Class** M7' Tank locomotive, number 30107, working a local two-coach auto-train near Bournemouth in August 1962. She continued working these local passenger trains until she was withdrawn from service at Bournemouth in May 1964. She was later scrapped. *(Photo © PC)*.

BR Standard 'Class 4/3' Tank locomotive, number 80036, pictured having arrived at Shorncliffe Station (now Folkestone West) in a shabby state, with a local passenger train service from Dover on 29 May 1961. *(Photo © PC).*

SR. (IOW). 'Class 02' Tank locomotive, number W29, *Alverstone*, pictured approaching Ryde Esplanade Station with a four coach evening passenger train service to Cowes on the Isle of Wight at the height of the holiday season in August 1965. *(Photo © PC).*

LMS (MR). 'Class 1F' Tank locomotive, number 41835, pictured performing shunting duties at Staverley Iron Works, Derbyshire, in the early 1960s. A shunter is walking alongside the engine, not wearing a shunter's uniform but carrying his shunting pole. *(Photo © PC).*

LMS. 'Class 2MT' Tank locomotive, number 41204, pictured arriving at Shrewsbury Station with a local passenger train service from Hartlebury near Kidderminster on 23 June 1962. A group of train-spotters are gathered at the end of platform five, to witness and record the event. *(Photo © PC).*

LNER (GNR).
'**Class** J6' locomotive, number 64277, pictured hauling an empty coach and two vans through Hemsworth, West Yorkshire, towards Doncaster on 28 May 1960. (Photo © PC).

LNER. 'Class A3' locomotive, number 60112, *St Simon*, pictured in steam outside York Shed in 1964, shortly before being withdrawn from service to be scrapped. (Photo © PC).

GWR 'Hall Class', mixed traffic locomotive, number 4932, *Hatherton Hall*, pictured hauling an up express goods train through Swindon Station in August 1963. *(Photo © PC).*

The final days of a shabby GWR 'Hall Class' locomotive, number 4958 *Priory Hall,* pictured here at Gloucester Shed in August 1964. She was withdrawn from service the following month and transported to Cashmore's Scrapyard in Newport, South Wales, where she was cut up. *(Photo © MC).*

SR. 'Q Class' locomotive, number 30541, pictured at Bournemouth locomotive shed in August 1962. The shed plate is missing from the smokebox door on the front of the locomotive. Although designated as freight locomotives (BR 4F), these engines were often called upon to perform passenger duties. *(Photo © PC).*

A sorry sight to see a former Southern Railway 'MN Class' elite express passenger locomotive, number 35012, *United States Line*, crawling tender-first through Wimbledon, having been reduced to working five empty wagons and two brake vans. This photograph was taken in 1965, two years before she was withdrawn from service in April 1967. She was later scrapped. *(Photo © PC).*

A well turned out LNER 'Class B1' locomotive, number 61049, pictured in steam outside York Shed in the 1960s, preparing to work an express freight train. Her shed plate, bearing the number 50A (York), is clearly visible on the smokebox door at the front of the locomotive. (Photo © PC).

LNER. 'Class B16/3' locomotive, number 61420, working a Class 'C', express freight, 'Banana Train' through Pontefract, West Yorkshire, in 1960. Almost all perishable foodstuffs and livestock being transported around the country was conveyed by train before the advent of the motorways at the end of the 1950s and into the 1960s. (Photo © PC).

LMS, 'Class 4F' locomotive, number 44411, pictured alongside a turntable at Templecombe Shed (SDR) in August 1963. Her shed plate, which is displayed on the front of the smokebox door, shows her home shed as being '82F' which at the time was Bath Green Park (SDR). *(Photo © MC).*

A stunning photograph of LMS 'Class 4F' locomotive, number 44082, hauling a passenger train through Ackworth, West Yorkshire, in 1960. These locomotives were designed exclusively for working freight but in later years they were also used for working passenger train services. *(Photo © PC).*

LMS, 'Class 4F' locomotive, number 44212, shows a visible presence as she hauls a passenger train service through the scenic countryside of Pontefract, West Yorkshire, in 1960. *(Photo © PC).*

SR. 'West Country Class' locomotive, number 34021, *Dartmoor,* is caught on camera in a side-view as she zips along with an express passenger train at Southampton in 1965. *(Photo © PC).*

Another photograph of SR 'WC Class' number 34021, *Dartmoor*. This time she is taking on water whilst working an express passenger train at Basingstoke in July 1964. The fireman standing on top of the tender shows little regard for health and safety. It was all part of a day's work. *(Photo © MC)*.

SR. 'West Country Class' (un-rebuilt) locomotive, number 34006, *Bude*, pictured hauling an express passenger train through Basingstoke in July 1963. *(Photo © MC)*.

SR. Un-rebuilt 'Battle of Britain Class' locomotive, number 34072, *257 Squadron,* pictured in May 1961, whilst working a London Waterloo to Padstow express through Wadebridge in Cornwall. In their early years, Battle of Britain locomotives would seldom venture into Cornwall. *(Photo © PC).*

Considered by many to be the most famous locomotive in the world. LNER, 'Class A3' locomotive, number 60103, *Flying Scotsman,* is pictured speeding non-stop through Selby Station, North Yorkshire, with the King's Cross to Newcastle down *Norseman* express passenger train on 17 August 1961. *(Photo © PC).*

Another photograph of *Flying Scotsman.* In this picture, she appears very different from the way she looks in the previous photograph. This picture shows her at Ardsley near Leeds in June 1962, fitted with the German type 'Witte' smoke deflectors as she hauls the *Queen of Scots* Pullman express from King's Cross to Glasgow, via Leeds Central, Harrogate and Edinburgh. *(Photo © PC).*

This side view photograph taken in the summer of 1963, shows GWR 'County Class' locomotive, number 1014, *County of Glamorgan*, at Cardiff General Station (now called Cardiff Central), coupled to a passenger train which was destined for Swansea. *(Photo © MC).*

GWR 'County Class' locomotive, number 1020, *County of Monmouth*, pictured leaving Abergavenny Monmouth Road Station with a Manchester bound passenger express in August 1963. *(Photo © PC).*

SR 'Schools Class' locomotive, number 30925, *Cheltenham*, pictured in front of LMS 'Class 2P' locomotive number 40646, double heading a Railway Correspondence & Travel Society rail tour at York Railway Station in April 1962. *(Photo © PC).*

Another SR 'Schools Class' locomotive, number 30935, *Sevenoaks,* is pictured here working a local passenger service through Sandling Junction in Kent on 9 June 1961. *(Photo © PC).*

LMS (SDJR). 'Class 7F' locomotive, number 53804, was built by the Midland Railway Company for use on the SDJR to haul heavy coal and goods trains. She was not intended to be used on passenger train services, although this photograph shows her at Bath Green Park Station being utilised for precisely that as she prepared to depart with a passenger train on 11 September 1960. *(Photo © PC).*

LMS. 'Class 7F' locomotive number 49618, pictured departing Pontefract Monkhill Station, West Yorkshire, with a Knottingley to Wakefield short goods train on 8 April 1961. *(Photo © PC)*.

LNER 'Class J50' Tank locomotive, number 68934, and LNER 'Class L1' Tank locomotive, number 67759, both engaged in shunting duties at the former GNR goods yard at Batley, West Yorkshire, in April 1961. The goods yard and a large part of the station closed in 1964. *(Photo © PC)*.

BR Standard 'Class 9F' locomotive, number 92138, pictured hauling a heavy freight train through Pontefract, West Yorkshire, in 1965. *(Photo © PC)*.

BR Standard 'Class 9F' locomotive, number 92203, pictured working a down iron-ore train through Grange Court Junction, Gloucestershire, in August 1964. *(Photo © MC)*.

BR Standard 'Class 9F' heavy freight locomotive, number 92239, pictured outside York Shed in 1960, fired up and ready for use. This side-on view displays the sheer size of this 100 ton monster, incorporating her 2-10-0 wheel arrangement and double chimney. *(Photo © PC)*.

GWR '4200 Class' Tank locomotive, number 4285 (shed plate missing), pictured at Pontypridd working one of the last steam hauled coal trains from the South Wales Valleys in mid-April 1965. She was withdrawn from service just two weeks later and scrapped. *(Photo © PC)*.

GWR '5101 Class' Tank locomotive, number 4169, and numerous other tank engines stabled outside Radyr locomotive shed near Cardiff in June 1965. All these engines had been withdrawn from service and were destined for the scrapyard. Radyr Shed itself closed the following month. *(Photo © MC).*

LNER 'Class 04/6' locomotive, number 63920, pictured at Hemsworth, West Yorkshire, whilst working a 'Class E' ballast train from Scunthorpe on 21 June 1960. *(Photo © PC).*

The locomotive scrapping programme continues as LNER 'Class 02/2', number 63946, awaits her fate, along with numerous other engines outside Doncaster Shed in 1963. All have been withdrawn from service for scrap. 63946 was later cut up at Doncaster Locomotive Works. *(Photo © MC).*

An unidentified GWR 'Hall Class' locomotive hauls a goods train through Chalford, Gloucestershire, towards Sapperton Bank in August 1963. A GWR 'Class 6400' Pannier Tank engine number 6437, which forms part of the train, had recently been withdrawn from service and was being transported to Swindon Works where she was cut up for scrap the following month. *(Photo © PC).*

GWR 'Hall Class' locomotive, number 5984 *Linden Hall*, pictured working a local passenger service at Gowerton North Station (GWR), near Swansea, on 16 August 1960. Gowerton North was later re-named Gowerton Station after Gowerton South (LMS/LNWR) station closed in 1964. *(Photo © PC)*.

SR. 'Merchant Navy Class' locomotive, number 35004, *Cunard White Star*, pictured at Templecombe Upper Station, whilst working an express passenger service in August 1963. *(Photo © MC)*.

SR. Un-rebuilt 'Battle of Britain Class' locomotive, number 34089, *602 Squadron*, pictured arriving at Folkestone Central Station with the down Golden Arrow express on 22 June 1960. *(Photo © PC).*

LMS. 'Class 3F' Tank locomotive, number 47631, pictured at Skipton in 1964. Although designed and built for freight, she was fitted with push and pull apparatus for passenger work. *(Photo © PC).*

LMS. 'Class 3F'
Tank locomotive, number 47295, pictured performing pilot duties at Carlisle Station in August 1964. These locomotives were usually referred to as 'Jinty' engines.
(Photo © MC).

This impressive photograph shows an LMS 'Jubilee Class' locomotive, number 45564 *New South Wales*, departing Pontefract Baghill with a southbound express in 1962.
(Photo © PC).

LMS. Unidentified 'Jubilee Class' locomotive, hauling an express passenger train along a long straight stretch of track near the rural town of High Bentham, North Yorkshire, in the 1960s. *(Photo © PC).*

LNER (NBR). 'Class J36' locomotive, number 65345. Pictured in steam as a light engine outside Thornton Junction Shed, Fife, Scotland, on 29 August 1964. *(Photo © PC).*

LNER (NBR). 'Class J36' locomotive, number 65224, *Mons*, pictured outside Seafield Shed, Edinburgh, on 5 May 1960. This locomotive was shipped to France during the First World War and given her name to commemorate the battle of Mons upon her return to Scotland. *(Photo © PC)*.

LNER. 'Class V2' mixed traffic locomotive, number 60895, pictured working an up goods train through Colton, North Yorkshire, in 1964. *(Photo © PC)*.

Another LNER 'Class V2' locomotive, number 60859. This mixed traffic locomotive is working an ordinary passenger service through Hemsworth, West Yorkshire, in 1960. Although sporting a single chimney, she was fitted with a double chimney shortly after this picture was taken. *(Photo © PC).*

This stunning picture shows the summer sun setting on Treherbert Railway Station in the Rhondda Valley, South Wales, as the daily parcels train arrives from Cardiff in the summer of 1962. The parcels train is being hauled by a GWR 'Class 5600' Tank locomotive, number 6689. *(Photo © MC).*

GWR '4200 Class' Tank locomotive, number 4268, pictured in steam outside Llantrisant Locomotive Shed in March 1963. Llantrisant shed (88G) closed in October 1964 and number 4268 moved to Ebbw Junction Shed at Newport until being withdrawn from service in August 1965. *(Photo © MC)*.

GWR '5101 Class' Large Prairie Tank locomotive, number 4100, pictured at Gloucester Central Station in August 1964. 140 of these medium sized tank locomotives were built at Swindon Works over a twenty year period between 1929 and 1949. *(Photo © MC)*.

GWR Pannier Tank, number 3759, pictured on Weymouth Quay in August 1962 with a young boy looking spellbound by the event. A branch line, called the Weymouth Harbour Tramway, connects the GWR main-line to Weymouth Quay Station but it has rarely been used since 1987. *(Photo © PC).*

BR 'Class WD' locomotive, number 90610, captured on camera hauling a mixed goods train past Locke's Sidings, Normanton, West Yorkshire, in 1965. *(Photo © PC).*

BR 'Class WD' locomotive, number 90488, pictured hauling empty coal wagons at Upton Colliery, West Yorkshire, in 1964. Although the locomotive appears to be in excellent condition, she was withdrawn from service a few months later and subsequently scrapped. *(Photo © PC).*

BR Standard 'Class 5MT' locomotive, number 73085 *Melisande,* pictured working a goods train, mainly consisting of tankers, through Wimbledon in 1965. The name *Melisande* was transferred to this locomotive from a SR 'King Arthur Class' locomotive which was withdrawn for scrap in 1959. *(Photo © PC).*

BR Standard 'Class 5MT' locomotive, number 73086 *The Green Knight*, pictured working a passenger/parcels train at Templecombe Upper Station in August 1963. The name *The Green Knight* was transferred to this locomotive from a SR 'King Arthur Class' locomotive which was withdrawn for scrap in 1959. *(Photo © MC)*.

GWR 'Grange Class' Locomotive, number 6823 *Oakley Grange*, pictured as a light engine outside Severn Tunnel locomotive shed on 3 June 1963. She was eventually withdrawn from service in May 1965 and cut up at Birds Scrapyard, Long Marston, Warwickshire, in November 1965. *(Photo © MC)*.

GWR 'Grange Class' locomotive, number 6873 *Caradoc Grange*, produces an abundance of black smoke as she hauls an up-express freight train near Church Stretton, Shropshire, in April 1963. *(Photo © PC).*

LMS, 'Jubilee Class' locomotive, number 45648 *Wemyss,* pictured working a passenger train service at Pontefract Baghill Station, West Yorkshire, in 1961. *(Photo © PC).*

GWR '5600 Class' Tank locomotive number 5613, pictured in July 1964, at Treherbert, Rhondda, having recovered a broken down diesel multiple unit which is being towed into the diesel sidings. *(Photo © MC).*

LNER. 'Class K3/2' locomotive, number 61814, pictured working a goods train through Goole Station, East Yorkshire, in 1960. She was withdrawn from service in December 1961 and later scrapped. *(Photo © PC).*

LNER. 'Class 02/3' locomotive, number 63973, pictured at Retford Shed in August 1962. She was in a sorry state with her cab-side number worn away. Despite her derelict appearance, she was still in service and continued to work for over a year before being withdrawn for scrap. *(Photo © MC).*

SR. 'Class U' locomotive, number 31802, pictured working a local passenger service at Templecombe in August 1963. She continued working for just over a year before being withdrawn for scrap in September 1964. *(Photo © MC).*

SR. 'Class Q1'
Austerity locomotive, number 33020, pictured hauling a freight train through Basingstoke in July 1964. She remained in service until January 1966 before being withdrawn for scrap. *(Photo © MC).*

GWR '2251 Class'
locomotive, number 2253, pictured working a local goods train through Ross-on-Wye, Herefordshire, from the direction of Lydbrook Junction in August 1964. *(Photo © PC).*

GWR 'Class 4300' locomotive number 6365, pictured working a Hereford to Gloucester local passenger service at Ross-on-Wye in August 1963. *(Photo © PC).*

LNER. 'Class K1' unidentified locomotive, pictured at Moorthorpe Station, West Yorkshire, heading tender first, south towards Frickley Colliery with empty coal wagons in 1965. *(Photo © PC).*

SR. Rebuilt 'Battle of Britain Class' locomotive, number 34085, *501 Squadron*, pictured at Templecombe Station in August 1963 with an express passenger train. *(Photo © MC)*.

A grubby looking BR Standard 'Class 9F' locomotive, number 92026, emitting an abundance of dirty black smoke, as she hauls an up train of empty wagons through York Holgate in 1964. 92026 was originally fitted with a Crosti experimental boiler which was later removed. *(Photo © PC)*.

SR. Rebuilt 'West Country Class' locomotive, number 34028 *Eddystone,* pictured having been demoted to work an up goods train through Upway near Weymouth in August 1962. In May 1964, she was the first rebuilt Bullied light pacific to be withdrawn for scrap but was later rescued from the scrapyard and is now preserved on the Swanage Heritage Railway in Dorset. *(Photo © PC).*

LNER. 'Class B1' locomotive number 61304, departing Pontefract Baghill Station, with a Scarborough to Sheffield Victoria, Saturday only, returning seaside excursion train in the summer of 1960. These ten coach seaside specials were abundant in the 1950s and early 1960s, conveying passengers to the east coast resorts of Whitby, Scarborough, Bridlington and Filey in their thousands. *(Photo © PC).*

LNER 'Class K1' locomotive number 62059, pictured working a freight train through York Holgate on 20 August 1964. Her shed plate 51A (Darlington) is clearly visible on the smokebox door. A similar plate is fitted beneath, displaying the initials 'SC' (Self Cleaning) which indicates that the locomotive is fitted with apparatus which gives the locomotive a 'self-cleaning smokebox'. *(Photo © MC)*.

LMS. 'Class 3F' Tank locomotive, number 47325, pictured at Derby Midland Station in 1964. She continued in service until September 1965 when she was withdrawn for scrap. *(Photo © MC)*.

LMS. 'Class 3F' Tank locomotive, number 47667, pictured at Carlisle Station in 1965 whilst shunting passenger coaches. She remained in service until the end of November 1966. *(Photo © MC).*

LNER. 'Class A3' locomotive, number 60062 *Minoru,* looking tired and neglected as she prepares for another hard day's work at York Shed in 1964. This was her final year in service. *(Photo © PC).*

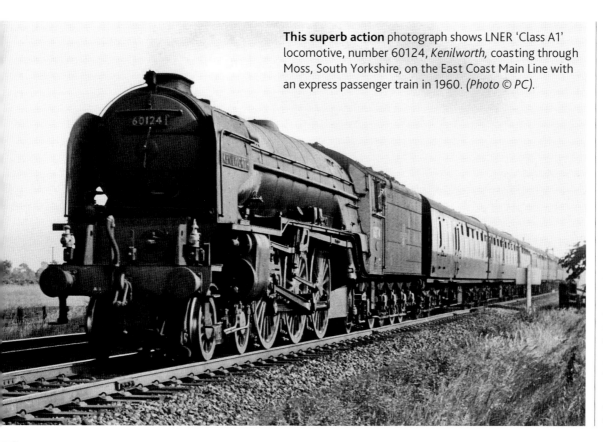

This superb action photograph shows LNER 'Class A1' locomotive, number 60124, *Kenilworth,* coasting through Moss, South Yorkshire, on the East Coast Main Line with an express passenger train in 1960. *(Photo © PC).*

GWR 'Class 1400' Tank locomotive, number 1474, pictured at Gloucester Shed in August 1964. The letters G W, from the original 'GWR' lettering, can be seen showing through the dilapidated post-war British Railways paintwork, although the early (pre 1956) BR 'lion on wheel' emblem is still clearly visible. *(Photo © MC).*

GWR 'Class 1400' Tank locomotive, number 1440, pictured at Chalford Station, having worked the single coach, local auto-train passenger service from Gloucester in August 1963. The service was discontinued the following year and Chalford Station was closed on 2 November 1964. *(Photo © PC)*.

BR. Standard 'Britannia Class' locomotive, number 70013, *Oliver Cromwell,* pictured working a Newcastle to Bournemouth express passenger train through West Yorkshire on 23 July 1960. Three cooling towers from Ferrybridge 'B' Power Station are just visible on the horizon, they have since been demolished. The viaduct beneath is the three arch railway bridge in Pontefract. *(Photo © PC)*.

Another 'Britannia Class' mixed traffic locomotive. In this picture, number 70002, *Geoffrey Chaucer*, is travelling on the up express track non-stop through Selby Station, North Yorkshire, with a York to Whitemoor (Cambridgeshire) express goods train on 22 August 1961. *(Photo © PC)*.

BR. Standard 'Britannia Class' mixed traffic locomotive, number 70049 *Solway Firth*, pictured at Dewsbury Wellington Road Station whilst working a Stockport to Leeds parcels train in 1964. The locomotive was in a very shabby condition with the nameplates having been removed. *(Photo © PC)*.

BR Standard 'Clan Class' locomotive, number 72008, *Clan MacLeod*, pictured as a light engine at Carlisle on 12 August 1964. *(Photo © MC)*.

GWR 'Grange Class' locomotive, number 6835, *Eastham Grange*, pictured in August 1962 at Upwey in Dorset, whilst working a local all stations passenger service to Weymouth. The shed plate is missing from the smokebox door on the front of the locomotive. *(Photo © PC)*.

Another GWR 'Grange Class' locomotive. In this picture, number 6838, *Goodmoor Grange*, pictured in North Wales, working an up express goods train through Ruabon Station near Wrexham in July 1962. *(Photo © PC)*.

A powerful rebuilt 'Merchant Navy Class' Pacific locomotive, number 35023, *Holland-Afrika Line*, arrives at her destination on time as she pulls into London Waterloo Station with an up express passenger service in the mid-1960s. *(Photo © PC)*.

Another SR rebuilt 'Merchant Navy Class' locomotive, number 35012, *United States Line*, is caught on camera performing humble duties for an express passenger locomotive, as she hauls a short train of empty wagons through Wimbledon, South-West London, in 1965. *(Photo © PC)*.

GWR design (BR built). 'Class 9400' Pannier tank, number 8400, pictured at Gloucester Shed in August 1964. The smokebox number plate and shed plate have been removed, no doubt in readiness for her withdrawal from service the following month. She was later scrapped. *(Photo © MC)*.

GWR design (BR built). 'Class 9400' Pannier tank locomotive, number 9437, pictured hauling a down (westbound) goods train through Cardiff in the summer of 1964. The engine is in a grubby state and the shed plate has been removed from the front of the locomotive. *(Photo © MC).*

LNER 'Class J38' locomotive, number 65923, pictured hauling coal wagons out of the railway sidings at New Mills Power Station, Kincardine, Fife, Scotland, on 17 June 1960. *(Photo © PC).*

LNER. 'Class V2' locomotive number 60930, arriving at Leeds Central Station with a local passenger service from Doncaster in 1961. Leeds Central Station closed on 1 May 1967. *(Photo © PC).*

The last days of steam for this BR 'Class WD' locomotive, number 90339, pictured working a mixed goods train (which includes a military army tank) through Normanton, West Yorkshire, just prior to being withdrawn from service in July 1967. She was scrapped by Drapers of Hull. *(Photo © PC).*

BR Standard 'Class 4MT' locomotive, number 75007, arriving at Templecombe Lower Station with a local passenger service to Bath Green Park on the former Somerset and Dorset Railway (line now closed) in August 1963. *(Photo © MC)*.

BR Standard 'Class 5MT' locomotive, number 73015, pictured working a passenger service through Pontefract, West Yorkshire, in 1960. *(Photo © PC)*.

Another BR Standard 'Class 5MT' locomotive working many miles away in Scotland. Number 73062 is pictured at Stonehaven Station in Aberdeenshire, whilst working the 9.40am Aberdeen to Perth passenger train service on 17 June 1962. *(Photo © PC).*

A well turned out 'Battle of Britain Class' (rebuilt) locomotive, number 34088, *213 Squadron*, is seen here working an express passenger train through Templecombe in August 1963. *(Photo © MC).*

GWR 'Class 5700' Pannier tank locomotive, number 9651, based locally at Cardiff East Dock shed, is pictured hauling a mixed freight train, westbound through Cardiff in 1963. A grand total of 863 of these successful and versatile pannier tanks were built for light goods work but were later used for shunting and pilot duties as well as working local passenger services. *(Photo © MC).*

Another of these popular GWR 'Class 5700' Pannier Tank engines, number 3760, pictured at Ruabon in North Wales whilst working the 3.58pm Wrexham to Bala local passenger service in July 1962. *(Photo © PC).*

SR. 'Class A1X' Tank locomotive, number 32646, pictured having arrived at Hayling Island Station with a local passenger train from Havant on 13 May 1961. *(Photo © PC).*

SR (LSWR). 'Class T9' locomotive number 30313, pictured arriving at Wadebridge, Cornwall, in May 1961, with a local passenger and parcels train from Padstow. She was withdrawn from service just two months later and scrapped in September 1961. Padstow station closed in 1967. *(Photo © PC).*

This unidentified BR 2-6-0 Standard 'Class 2' locomotive is pictured at Grange Court Station, Gloucestershire, whilst working a Hereford to Gloucester passenger train service on 26 September 1964. The station closed just five weeks later and was subsequently demolished. *(Photo © MC).*

BR Standard 'Class 4/3' Tank locomotive, number 80050, working a single coach parcels train at Ayr in Scotland on 26 May 1961. *(Photo © PC).*

A spectacular sight with billows of smoke as the sun sets on 'Britannia Class' locomotive, number 70022, *Tornado,* pictured here leaving Skipton, North Yorkshire, with a Leeds to Glasgow express on 24 April 1962. *(Photo © PC).*

Another photograph taken near Skipton in North Yorkshire as LNER 'Class A3' locomotive, number 60069, *Sceptre*, works a passenger train through the hamlet of Bell Busk on the Leeds to Morecambe line in the early 1960s. *(Photo © PC)*.

LMS, 'Class 4F' locomotive, number 44265, pictured hauling an express passenger train through Pontefract in 1960. It was not uncommon to see these freight locomotives being used to work passenger services at this time. *(Photo © PC)*.

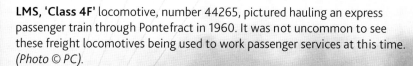

Another photograph of an LMS 0-6-0, 'Class 4F'. This time locomotive number 44137 is performing duties that she was designed and built for as she hauls a slow goods train non-stop through Gloucester Central Station in the summer of 1964. *(Photo © MC)*.

LNER. 'Class V2' locomotive, number 60867, pictured at Moss, South Yorkshire, in 1960, working an express freight train of seed potatoes from Whitemoor, Cambridgeshire, to Edinburgh. *(Photo © PC)*.

Another LNER 'Class V2' locomotive. Number 60929 is pictured taking a short break from active duties as she sits in the sidings outside her home shed at York in the early 1960s. *(Photo © PC).*

BR Standard 'Class 9F' locomotive, number 92243, reveals her true size when compared with a GWR '2800 Class' number 2841 alongside her at Severn Tunnel Junction Shed on 3 June 1963. With the end of the steam era in sight and no need for banking assistance in the Severn Tunnel for diesel locomotives, this busy engine shed closed down in October 1965. *(Photo © MC).*

Another powerful BR Standard 'Class 9F' locomotive, number 92145, pictured hauling a flat wagon container train through Brayton near Selby, North Yorkshire, on 13 September 1961. *(Photo © PC).*

GWR 'Castle Class' locomotive, number 7001, *Sir James Milne*, steams into Shrewsbury Station with a Wolverhampton to Birkenhead passenger train in April 1963. *(Photo © PC).*

GWR 'Castle Class' locomotive, number 5085, *Evesham Abbey*, pictured at Cardiff General Station in June 1963, working a passenger train to Swansea. The smokebox number plate has been removed from the front of the locomotive, possibly by an overzealous souvenir hunter. *(Photo © MC)*.

This nice side view of an LNER 'Class B1' locomotive number 61018, taken at York in 1963, clearly displays her nameplate *Gnu*. This was unique, inasmuch as the name *Gnu* (named after a large African antelope) was the shortest name ever bestowed upon a British Steam Locomotive. *(Photo © PC)*.

Another LNER 'Class B1' locomotive is pictured working a passenger service at Ardsley near Leeds in 1961. Like the majority of 'Class B1' engines, number 61328 was un-named. *(Photo © PC)*.

LMS, 'Patriot Class' locomotive, number 45506, *The Royal Pioneer Corps*, pictured entering Pontefract Baghill Station with a heavy express passenger train in 1960, during the twilight years of her service. She was withdrawn from service and scrapped at Crewe Works in March 1962. *(Photo © PC)*.

LMS, 'Royal Scot Class' locomotive, number 46109, *Royal Engineer*, pictured at Wakefield Kirkgate in 1962, downgraded to pulling empty wagons. Despite her seemingly immaculate condition, she was withdrawn from service at the end of the year and later scrapped. *(Photo © PC)*.

LMS (Caledonian Railway) 'Class 2F' locomotive number 57378, seen here chugging along through the rural Scottish surroundings at Summerville, Dumfries, with a short mineral train on 20 May 1961. *(Photo © PC)*.

SR. Rebuilt 'Battle of Britain Class' locomotive, number 34087, *145 Squadron*, gathers speed as she heads out of London through Vauxhall with the 8.35am Waterloo to Bournemouth express passenger train on 27 June 1967. *(Photo © PC).*

SR. Un-rebuilt 'West Country Class' locomotive, number 34106, *Lydford*, seen here reduced to hauling a milk train through Clapham Junction, South London, in 1964. *(Photo © PC).*

SR. 'Merchant Navy Class' locomotive, number 35014, *Nederland Line*, pictured working an express passenger train at Basingstoke in July 1964. (Photo © MC).

BR Standard 'Class 5MT' locomotive, number 73018, pictured at Wareham Station, Dorset, whilst working a London, Waterloo to Weymouth passenger express on 5 June 1963. (Photo © PC).

Another BR Standard 'Class 5MT' locomotive working out of London Waterloo. On this occasion, number 73043 is pictured at Waterloo Station, preparing to depart for the South Coast with an express passenger train service in 1965. *(Photo © PC)*.

LMS, 'Jubilee Class' locomotive, number 45570, *New Zealand*, making her mark by displaying a fountain of smoke as she works an express passenger train through Pontefract, West Yorkshire, in 1960. *(Photo © PC)*.

LMS, 'Jubilee Class' locomotive, number 45596, *Bahamas,* pictured working a parcels train at Hest Bank, Morecambe, on 24 August 1961. Her 'double chimney' is clearly visible. Only five (out of 191) 'Jubilee Class' locomotives were fitted with double chimneys at various times. *Bahamas* received her double chimney in 1961 shortly before this picture was taken. *(Photo © PC).*

This picture taken in 1963 shows a bustling Treherbert Station in the famous Rhondda Valley, a valley built on coal. Within just six years, the engine sheds and steam locomotives had disappeared. The Rhondda Tunnel had closed and the coal trains were a thing of the past. The coal miners had moved on and pits were just a memory, confined to history. Truly the end of an era. *(Photo © MC).*

BR. Standard 'Britannia Class' locomotive, number 70015, *Apollo*, pictured departing the former Pontypool Road Station with a passenger express to Manchester in June 1964. Prior to the 1950s, Pontypool Road was one of the busiest railway junctions in the country. *(Photo © MC)*.

BR Standard 'Class 5MT' locomotive, number 73171, pictured working a southbound passenger train at Pontefract Baghill Station, West Yorkshire, in 1960. *(Photo © PC)*.

BR Standard 'Class 5MT' locomotive, number 73046, pictured working an express passenger train through Burton Salmon, North Yorkshire, in 1961. *(Photo © PC)*.

LMS 'Black Five' locomotive, number 44830, pictured working a 'City of Leicester Holiday Express' passenger excursion train through Pontefract, West Yorkshire, in the summer of 1960, undoubtedly heading to the north-east coastal holiday resort of Scarborough or Bridlington. *(Photo © PC)*.

This dirty 'Black Five' locomotive, number 45211, is pictured working a coal train through Mirfield, West Yorkshire, in 1965. *(Photo © MC)*.

LMS, 'Rebuilt Jubilee Class' locomotive, number 45735, *Comet*, pictured working a passenger train service at Preston in the 1960s. Only two 'Jubilee Class' locomotives were rebuilt, this locomotive and number 45736 *Phoenix* which is featured in the next picture. *(Photo © PC)*.

This picture shows one of only two 'rebuilt' LMS 'Jubilee Class' locomotives. Number 45736, *Phoenix*, is pictured at Carlisle Station working a passenger train in August 1964, during her last weeks of service. She was withdrawn from service on 26 September 1964 for scrap. *(Photo © MC).*

BR Standard 'Class 2MT' locomotive, number 78022, pictured working the 9.40am Sheffield Midland to York local passenger service through Pontefract, West Yorkshire, on 3 September 1960. She was withdrawn from service in September 1966 but was rescued from the scrapyard and later preserved. She is currently working on the Keighley and Worth Valley Heritage Railway. *(Photo © PC).*

BR Standard 'Class 4MT' locomotive, number 75051, pictured in tranquil surroundings as she conveys a short goods train through Skipton North Junction, North Yorkshire, in 1965. *(Photo © PC).*

BR Standard 'Class 5MT' locomotive, number 73068, pictured passing Pontefract Junction signal box, with a Birmingham to Newcastle passenger train service in 1960. The locomotive was based at Bristol, Barrow Road Shed (82E) and was one of a number of Western Region Standard Five locomotives to be painted green as opposed to black. *(Photo © PC).*

BR Standard 'Class 4MT' locomotive, number 75006, seen here passing through Cefn Junction, Ruabon near Wrexham, with an up express passenger train in July 1962. *(Photo © PC)*.

It is a melancholy sight for any avid steam enthusiast to see this LNER 'Class A4' locomotive number 60034 *Lord Faringdon*, working a slow goods train through Retford, Nottinghamshire, in 1962. Hauling empty wagons is certainly not the type of work she was either designed or intended for. *(Photo © PC)*.

In contrast to the previous photograph, this picture shows the world famous LNER 'Class A4' locomotive, number 60022, *Mallard*, hurtling along the East Coast Main Line whilst hauling the up *Anglo Scottish Car Carrier* through Moss, South Yorkshire, on 25 June 1960. *(Photo © PC).*

This picture shows another LNER 'Class A4' locomotive. In this photograph, number 60027, *Merlin*, races non-stop through Selby Station, North Yorkshire, with *The Elizabethan* up-express passenger train (non-stop from Edinburgh to King's Cross) in 1961. *(Photo © PC).*

LNER. 'Class A1/1' locomotive, number 60113, *Great Northern*, pictured working a Leeds to King's Cross express passenger train through Hemsworth, West Yorkshire, on 11 May 1960. This locomotive was unique, as it was the only 'Class A1/1' ever built. Sadly it was not preserved. *(Photo © PC)*.

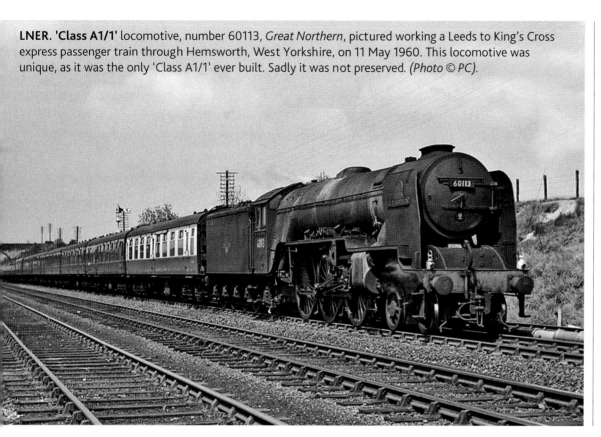

SR. 'Class LN' (Lord Nelson Class), locomotive number 30860, *Lord Hawke*, pictured working an up-express passenger train non-stop through Bournemouth Central on 24 April 1962. *(Photo © PC)*.

SR. 'Class N', mixed traffic locomotive, number 31873, is pictured hauling a short parcels train near Worting Junction, Basingstoke, in the mid-1960s not long before being withdrawn from service in January 1966. She was subsequently cut up for scrap. *(Photo © PC).*

LMS 'Patriot Class' locomotive, number 45504, *Royal Signals*, spouting black smoke as she passes from rural North Yorkshire into West Yorkshire between York and Sheffield with an express passenger service to Bristol in 1960. *(Photo © PC).*

LMS. 'Royal Scot Class' locomotive, number 46148, *The Manchester Regiment*, pictured at Crewe Railway Station on 2 August 1961, about to depart for London Euston with a passenger express. It is a delight to see the locomotive in such a pristine condition. *(Photo © PC)*.

GWR '5600 Class'. Tank locomotive number 5665, pictured with other locomotives, inside Treherbert (Rhondda) locomotive shed in 1963. The shed itself and all the locomotives were remarkably clean and tidy which, sadly, was an unfamiliar site at that time. A young boy train-spotter wearing short trousers can just be seen on the extreme right hand side of the picture. *(Photo © PC)*.

GWR 'Class 5700' Pannier Tank locomotive, number 9625, pictured working a goods train at the former Gowerton South (LNWR) Railway Station near Swansea on 16 August 1960. The station, which was originally built by the Llanelly Railway Company, closed in 1964. *(Photo © PC).*

SR (IOW). 'Class 02' Tank locomotive, number W24, *Calbourne*, pictured working an Isle of Wight passenger service near Ryde in the summer of 1965. The nameplates have been removed from the sides of the locomotive. *(Photo © PC).*

SR. (IOW). 'Class 02' Tank locomotive, number W30, *Shorwell*, pictured exiting Ventnor Tunnel with a passenger service from Ryde to Ventnor in August 1965. Ventnor Station, which was the terminus station of the Isle of Wight Railway line from Ryde, closed in April 1966 when stations south of Shanklin fell foul of the 'Beeching axe'. Ventnor tunnel was bricked up. *(Photo © PC).*

LMS. 'Class 8F' locomotive, number 48310, pictured giving off a huge amount of black smoke as she works her way west with a coal train through Mirfield, West Yorkshire, in August 1966. *(Photo © PC).*

LMS. 'Royal Scot Class' locomotive, number 46147, *The Northamptonshire Regiment*, working a Bristol to York express through Pontefract, Yorkshire, in 1960. On the right of the picture is an outer-home signal. This was an old NER wooden 'slotted arm' semaphore signal, a few of which were still in use at the time on the former Swinton & Knottingley Joint Railway section of the line. *(Photo © PC).*

One of the most popular and extremely efficient steam locomotives used by BR was the LMS 'Black Five'. In this picture, number 45290 is working a freight train through Skipton, North Yorkshire, in the summer of 1962. *(Photo © PC).*

Another 'Black Five' locomotive, number 45258, pictured at Wennington Station, Lancashire, in August 1965. On this occasion, the versatile mixed traffic locomotive is being utilised to work a passenger train service. A heavy cloud formation adds intensity to the photograph. *(Photo © MC).*

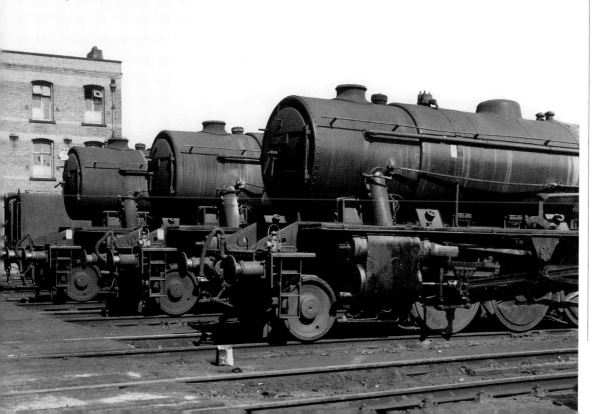

BR 'Class WD' locomotive, number 90047, pictured alongside other sister locomotives of the same class in this rather unusual photograph taken at Wakefield Shed in 1960. *(Photo © PC).*

This photograph shows a 'Class WD' locomotive, number 90540, in action as she hauls a heavy coal train through Thorne South Station, near Doncaster, South Yorkshire, in 1960. *(Photo © PC)*.

In this photograph, BR Standard 'Clan Class' locomotive, number 72009, *Clan Stewart*, is pictured at Apperley Bridge, West Yorkshire, effortlessly working a Glasgow to Leeds express on 29 July 1961. *(Photo © PC)*.

BR 'Class WD' locomotive, 90488, pictured at Upton Station, West Yorkshire, having just left Upton Colliery with a coal train in 1964. Upton Station, on the former Hull & Barnsley Railway, closed to passengers in 1932 but was still largely intact when this picture was taken. The nearby Upton Colliery closed in November 1964 for safety reasons after an explosion and was never re-opened. *(Photo © PC).*

GWR 'Castle Class' locomotive, number 5091, *Cleeve Abbey*, pictured at Swansea High Street Station, having worked the down South Wales *Pullman* express from Paddington on 16 August 1960. Swansea Landore Shed was the home base of this locomotive at the time, together with numerous other main line express passenger locomotives. *(Photo © PC).*

GWR design. 'Hall Class' locomotive, number 6982, *Melmerby Hall*, pictured at Newquay Station in Cornwall with a local passenger service from Par in May 1961. *(Photo © PC).*

LNER. 'Class K2/2' locomotive, number 61756, pictured on a turntable at Scarborough, having arrived earlier with a seaside excursion train from Normanton (Yorkshire) on 13 August 1960. This rare photograph shows the last ever visit by a 'Class K2/2' locomotive to Scarborough. *(Photo © PC).*

LNER 'Class K3/2' mixed traffic locomotive, number 61935, pictured working an express passenger train service through Goole, East Yorkshire, in 1960. *(Photo © PC)*.

SR 'Class Q1' locomotive number 33039, pictured departing Upwey Station in Dorset with a local stopping train service to Weymouth in 1962. The extraordinary design of these engines gave rise to them being referred to by such nicknames as 'Coffee Pots', 'Ugly Ducklings' and 'Charlies'. They were however extremely efficient and versatile austerity locomotives, built in 1942. *(Photo © PC)*.

These two sister locomotives, pictured at York Permanent Way Yard in 1965, were LNER 'Class J27', departmental locomotives, numbers 65844 and 65894. They were used by the railway authorities to haul regional maintenance trains all over the network to carry out civil engineering work on tracks, stations, bridges, etc. Number 65844 is in steam, manned and ready for use. *(Photo © PC)*.

This impressive photograph displays the power of LNER 'Class B16/1' locomotive, number 61436, as she hauls an express freight train through Pontefract, West Yorkshire, in 1960. *(Photo © PC)*.

LNER 'Class B1' locomotive, number 61329, pictured working a passenger train service through Ackworth cutting, West Yorkshire, in 1964. *(Photo © PC).*

BR. 'Class WD' locomotive, number 90633, pictured at Wakefield Shed, West Yorkshire, alongside an LNER 'Class B1', number 61303, in 1966. 61303 is displaying her shed plate number 50A which was York. Although the shed plate is missing from 90633, she was based at Wakefield. *(Photo © PC).*

LNER. 'Class A3' locomotive, number 60084, *Trigo*, pictured at Scarborough waiting to depart with the 9.20am Scarborough to Manchester express passenger train on 20 July 1963. Pacific locomotives seldom ventured to Scarborough, so this occasion was a rare but pleasant sight. *(Photo © PC).*

This photograph shows an LMS 'Black Five' locomotive, number 45495, meandering through the picturesque countryside near Wennington in Lancashire whilst working a Barrow to Leeds passenger train service on 7 August 1965. *(Photo © MC).*

Another stunning photograph of a 'Black Five' mixed traffic locomotive in action. Number 45104 is performing express freight duties in 1961, as she hauls a flat wagon container train down Hest Bank near Morecambe in Lancashire on the West Coast Main Line. *(Photo © PC)*.

A thirsty SR 'Class S15' locomotive, number 30832, is pictured taking on water at Templecombe Station on 19 August 1963 in what was to be her final year of service. 30832 was withdrawn from service the following January and subsequently scrapped. *(Photo © MC)*.

SR. 'Class S15' locomotive, number 30830, appears to be in remarkably good condition as she trundles through Templecombe Upper Station with a heavy ballast train on 19 August 1963. Despite her appearance, she was withdrawn from service less than a year later. *(Photo © MC)*.

The driver and fireman of this GWR '5700 Class' Pannier Tank locomotive, number 4689, look very relaxed having piloted a Channel Island boat train through Weymouth town towards Weymouth Quay Station in August 1962. The brass bell above the footplate was to warn pedestrians and motorists whilst the train was passing through the streets of Weymouth. *(Photo © PC)*.

LMS (MR). 'Class 0F' Tank locomotive, number 41533, pictured slowly pulling some empty wagons across the road at Staverley Iron Works, Derbyshire, in the early 1960s. *(Photo © PC).*

GWR 'Manor Class' locomotive, number 7815, *Fritwell Manor*, departs Grange Court Station with a local Hereford to Gloucester three coach passenger train on 26 September 1964. Despite local protests, Grange Court Station closed the following month on 31 October 1964. By a remarkable coincidence, *Fritwell Manor* was withdrawn from service on the exact same day. *(Photo © MC).*

This picture shows two GWR 'Class 2251' locomotives, numbers 2286 and 3208, double-heading a train through Cefn Junction, Ruabon, near Wrexham, in July 1962. The train in question was the 11.05am Pwllheli to Paddington passenger train. *(Photo © PC)*.

LMS (LYR). 'Class 21'. Saddle Tank 'Pug' locomotive, number 51244, pictured shunting a couple of empty wagons at Goole Docks in 1960. The shunter can be seen 'hitching a ride' on the steps of the engine which was common practice before the advent of health and safety. *(Photo © PC)*.

LNER. 'Class J72' Tank locomotive, number 68726, pictured entering Castleford Goods Yard, West Yorkshire in 1960 with a short goods train consisting of two brake vans and three sulphuric acid tanker wagons from the nearby Laporte Chemical Works (now closed). *(Photo © PC).*

The last steam locomotive ever built for BR was a 'Class 9F' number 92220, *Evening Star,* pictured here at Templecombe Upper Station on 19 August 1963, whilst working a passenger train from Bournemouth to Bath Green Park. This famous locomotive marked the end of steam and the end of an era. *Evening Star* is now on public display at the National Railway Museum in York. *(Photo © MC).*

LOCOMOTIVE TECHNICAL DETAILS AND ADDITIONAL INFORMATION

LOCOMOTIVE WHEEL CONFIGURATION.
Wheel configuration or wheel arrangement describes the way in which the distribution of locomotive wheels (wheel assembly) are counted. Several different methods have been used worldwide but the method adopted in Britain and Ireland (also the USA and Canada) for use on steam locomotives was the 'Whyte System' or 'Whyte Notation'.

The system consisted of three digits, separated by hyphens, e.g. 4-6-0, 2-6-2, 0-8-0. The three sets of numbers represent the order in which the wheels are arranged, starting at the front of the locomotive. They represent the number of leading wheels, the number of coupled driving wheels and the number of trailing wheels. Tender wheels are not included.

Tank engines did not have a tender for carrying water and coal. Coal was carried in a bunker behind the cab and water was carried in various styles of tank, the most common being side tanks, which were fitted to each side of the boiler (ordinary/side tank engine). Other types most commonly used were saddle tanks, pannier tanks and well tanks. The wheel configuration number also revealed if the locomotive was a tank engine, and the type of tank engine. This was indicated by using a suffix, e.g. 2-6-4T (ordinary tank engine), 0-6-0PT (pannier tank engine), 0-6-0ST (saddle tank engine), etc.

LOCOMOTIVES FEATURED IN THIS BOOK (IN NUMERICAL ORDER).

GREAT WESTERN RAILWAY LOCOMOTIVES.
No. 1014. *County of Glamorgan*. GWR. 4-6-0. 'Class 1000' (County Class) locomotive. Built at Swindon in February 1946 as GWR number 1014 (later BR 1014). Withdrawn from service in April 1964 and scrapped in December 1964. (Photo P.32).

No. 1020. *County of Monmouth*. GWR. 4-6-0. 'Class 1000' (County Class) locomotive. Built at Swindon in December 1946 as GWR number 1020 (later BR 1020). Withdrawn from service in February 1964 and scrapped in July 1964. (Photo P.33).

'Class 1000' (County Class) - Additional information.
A total of thirty 'County Class' locomotives, designed by Frederick Hawksworth, were built at Swindon between 1945 and 1947. They were designed and built as mixed traffic locomotives (BR power classification 6MT). They were frequently

used for working passenger train services but were extremely well suited for express freight services. Unfortunately, none was preserved. However, a replica of locomotive number 1014 *County of Glamorgan* (featured in this book), is now under construction at the Didcot Railway Centre, home of the Great Western Society. Construction of the boiler is expected to be completed sometime in 2020.

No. 1440. GWR. 0-4-2T. 'Class 1400' Tank locomotive. Built at Swindon in March 1935 as GWR number 1440 (later BR 1440). Withdrawn from service in December 1963 and scrapped in February 1964. (Photo P.60).

No. 1455. GWR. 0-4-2T. 'Class 1400' Tank locomotive. Built at Swindon in July 1935 as GWR number 1455 (later BR 1455). Withdrawn from service in May 1964 and scrapped in July 1964. (Photo P.20).

No. 1474. GWR. 0-4-2T. 'Class 1400' Tank locomotive. Built at Swindon in April 1936 as GWR number 1474 (later BR 1474). Withdrawn from service in September 1964 and scrapped in December 1964. (Photo P.59).

'Class 1400'- Additional information. A total of seventy-five 'Class 1400' tank engines were built and designed by Charles Collett to work light passenger trains on branch lines. They were fitted with push and pull apparatus for Auto-Train working. In 1948, they were given a BR power classification of 1P. Withdrawals started in 1956 with the introduction of Diesel Multiple Units.

No. 2253. GWR. 0-6-0. 'Class 2251' locomotive. Built at Swindon in March 1930 as GWR number 2253 (later BR 2253). Withdrawn from service in March 1965 and scrapped in May 1965. (Photo P.53).

No. 2286. GWR. 0-6-0. 'Class 2251' locomotive. Built at Swindon in January 1936 as GWR number 2286 (later BR 2286). Withdrawn from service in September 1964 and scrapped in January 1965. (Photo P.108).

'Class 2251' - Additional information. A total of 120 'Class 2251' locomotives designed by Charles Collett were built at Swindon Works between 1930 and 1948. They were designed to replace the Armstrong & Dean goods locomotives operating predominantly in Central Wales. 'Class 2251' locomotives were mixed traffic locomotives designed to haul medium powered freight trains and branch line passenger services (BR Power classification 3MT).

No. 2841. GWR. 2-8-0. 'Class 2800' locomotive. Built at Swindon in October 1912 as GWR number 2841 (later BR 2841). Withdrawn from service in December 1963 and scrapped in December 1964. (Photo P.75).

'Class 2800' - Additional information. A total of eighty-four 'Class 2800' 2-8-0 locomotives were built at Swindon between 1903 and 1919. They were designed by George Jackson Churchward as heavy freight locomotives (BR power classification 8F). The first member of the class (prototype) was built in 1903 as GWR number 97 but it was re-numbered 2800 in 1905 when production of the second and subsequent members of the class commenced.

The '2800 Class' locomotives were powerful and efficient and the whole class continued working well into the BR era. Withdrawals started in 1958 and the last member of the class, number 2876, was withdrawn from service in January 1965 before being cut up at Cashmores Scrapyard in Newport the following month.

No. 3208. GWR. 0-6-0. 'Class 2251' locomotive. Built at Swindon in September 1946 as GWR number 3208 (later BR 3208). Withdrawn from service in May 1965 and scrapped in August 1965. (Photo P.108).

No.3759. GWR. 0-6-0PT. 'Class 5700' Pannier Tank locomotive. Built at Swindon in December 1937 as GWR number 3759 (later BR 3759). Withdrawn from service in December 1965 and scrapped in April 1966. (Photo P.47).

No. 3760. GWR. 0-6-0PT. 'Class 5700' Pannier Tank locomotive. Built at Swindon in December 1937 as GWR number 3760 (later BR 3760). Withdrawn from service in September 1962 and scrapped in November 1962. (Photo P.70).

'Class 5700' – Additional information. A total of 863 'Class 5700' Pannier Tank locomotives, designed by Charles Collett, were built between 1929 and 1950. Originally designed as light goods and shunting engines, they were also extensively used for working local passenger services.

No. 4082. *Windsor Castle*. GWR. 4-6-0. 'Class 4073' (Castle) Class locomotive. Built at Swindon in April 1924 as GWR number 4082 (later BR 4082). Withdrawn from service in September 1964 and scrapped in January 1965. (Photo P.12).

'Class 4073' (Castle Class) – Additional information. A total of 171 'Class 4073' (Castle Class) locomotives were built at Swindon between 1923 and 1950. They were designed by Charles Collett as express passenger locomotives and a development of the highly successful GWR 'Class 4000' (Star Class) locomotives. When introduced, they were the most powerful express passenger locomotives in Britain (BR power classification 7P). They were well liked by the crews and turned out to be extremely successful locomotives. A total of eight were subsequently preserved.

No. 4100. GWR. 2-6-2T. 'Class 5101' (Large Prairie) Tank locomotive. Built at Swindon in August 1935 as GWR number 4100 (later BR 4100). Withdrawn from service in October 1965 and scrapped in February 1966. (Photo P.46).

No. 4169. GWR. 2-6-2T. 'Class 5101' (Large Prairie) Tank locomotive. Built at Swindon in November 1948 as GWR number 4169 (later BR 4169). Withdrawn from service in May 1965 and scrapped in June 1965. (Photo P.38).

'Class 5101' (Large Prairie Tanks) – Additional information. A total of 140 'Class 5101' Tank locomotives were built at Swindon between 1929 and 1949. They were designed by Charles Collett and although they were given the name 'Large Prairie Tanks' (as opposed to small prairie tanks), they were in fact medium-sized tank engines. These locomotives were classified as mixed traffic locomotives (BR, 4MT) and could be seen all over the former GWR system working local passenger services. They were also ideally suited and frequently used as banking engines and for shunting duties.

No. 4268. GWR. 2-8-0T. 'Class 4200' Tank locomotive. Built at Swindon in November 1919 as GWR number 4268 (later BR 4268). Withdrawn from service in August 1965 and scrapped in December 1965. (Photo P.46).

No. 4285. GWR. 2-8-0T. 'Class 4200' Tank locomotive. Built at Swindon in August 1920 as GWR number 4285 (later BR 4285). Withdrawn from service in April 1965 and scrapped in September 1965. (Photo P.37).

'Class 4200' – Additional information. A total of 105 'Class 4200' Tank locomotives were built at Swindon Works between 1910 and 1923. They were designed by G. J. Churchward as a development of his 'Class 2800' locomotive. The 'Class 4200' locomotives were large powerful tank engines (BR power classification 7F), specifically designed to work heavy coal trains on the steep inclines and sharp curves of the South Wales Valleys. Fourteen members of this class were later rebuilt as GWR '7200 Class' locomotives. Five members of the class have been preserved.

No. 4623. GWR. 0-6-0PT. 'Class 5700' Pannier Tank locomotive. Built at Swindon in June 1942 as GWR number 4623 (later BR 4623). Withdrawn from service in June 1965 and scrapped in October 1965. (Photo P.20).

No.4689. GWR. 0-6-0PT. 'Class 5700' Pannier Tank locomotive. Built at Swindon in December 1944 as GWR number 4689 (later BR 4689). Withdrawn from service in December 1965 and scrapped in April 1966. (Photo P.106).

No. 4932 *Hatherton Hall*. GWR. 4-6-0. 'Class 4900' (Hall Class) locomotive. Built at Swindon in June 1929 as GWR number 4932 (later BR 4932). Withdrawn from service in November 1964 and scrapped in April 1965. (Photo P.25).

No. 4958. *Priory Hall*. GWR. 4-6-0. 'Class 4900' (Hall Class) locomotive. Built at Swindon in September 1929 as GWR number 4958 (later BR 4958). Withdrawn from service in September 1964 and scrapped in January 1965. (Photo P.25).

'Class 4900' (Hall Class) – Additional information.
A total of 259 'Class 4900' (Hall Class) locomotives were built at Swindon Works between 1928 and 1943. They were designed by Charles Collett and purpose built exclusively for use as mixed traffic locomotives (BR Classification, 5 MT). They were the forerunners of the LMS Stanier Black Five, LNER Thompson B1 and BR Standard 5 mixed traffic locomotives.

'Class 4900' (Hall Class) locomotives and the later 'Class 6959' (Modified Hall Class) were all named after English and Welsh large country and medieval houses usually with landed estates.

No. 5060. *Earl of Berkeley*. GWR. 4-6-0. 'Class 4073' (Castle Class) locomotive. Built at Swindon in June 1937 as GWR number 5060 (later BR 5060). Withdrawn from service in April 1963 and scrapped in March 1964. Number 5060 was originally named *Sarum Castle* when she entered service in June 1937. She was re-named *Earl of Berkeley* in October of that year (1937). (Photo P.12).

No. 5085. *Evesham Abbey*. GWR. 4-6-0. 'Class 4073' (Castle Class) locomotive. Built at Swindon in July 1939 as GWR number 5085 (later BR 5085). Withdrawn from service in February 1964 and scrapped in June 1964.

Number 5085 was originally built in 1922 as a GWR 'Class 4000' (Star Class) locomotive number 4065. She was given the name *Evesham Abbey*. In July 1939, she was rebuilt as a 'Class 4073' (Castle Class) locomotive. She retained her original name, *Evesham Abbey*, but was re-numbered 5085, which she retained for the remainder of her service. (Photo P.77).

No. 5091. *Cleeve Abbey*. GWR. 4-6-0. 'Class 4073' (Castle Class) locomotive. Built at Swindon in December 1938 as GWR number 5091 (later BR 5091). Withdrawn from service in October 1964 and scrapped in November 1964.

Number 5091 was originally built in February 1923 as a GWR 'Class 4000' (Star Class) locomotive number 4071. She was given the name *Cleeve Abbey*. In December 1938, she was rebuilt as a 'Class 4073' (Castle Class) locomotive. She retained her original name *Cleeve Abbey* but was re-numbered 5091, which she retained for the remainder of her service. (Photo P.99).

No. 5613. GWR. 0-6-2T. 'Class 5600' Tank locomotive. Built at Swindon in February 1925 as GWR number 5613 (later BR 5613). Withdrawn from service in May 1965 and scrapped in August 1965. (Photo P.51).

No. 5665. GWR. 0-6-2T. 'Class 5600' Tank locomotive. Built at Swindon in June 1926 as GWR number 5665 (later BR 5665). Withdrawn from service in June 1965 and scrapped in August 1965. (Photo P.93).

'Class 5600' – Additional information.
A total of 150 'Class 5600' Tank locomotives were built at Swindon Works and an additional fifty by Armstrong Whitworth of Newcastle (grand total = 200), between 1924 and 1928. These 0-6-2T locomotives were designed by Charles B. Collett to be used by the newly created GWR, as a standard type tank engine, to replace a large and varied collection of engines inherited from various

Welsh Railway Companies after the 1923 railway groupings.

Most of these inherited locomotives were in good condition but nevertheless, they were scrapped as they did not fit in to the GWR standardisation programme, with the exception of a number of former Taff Vale Railway locomotives, which were absorbed into the GWR stock. Many of these former Taff Vale engines remained in service until the 1950s. The replacement 'Class 5600' locomotives continued operating into the 1960s. They were all withdrawn from BR service between 1962 and 1965. Nine have been preserved.

Although the 'Class 5600' locomotives were in service for many years, they were never considered to be a very successful locomotive. They were not well liked by the train crews and were prone to mechanical failures. In particular, they frequently experienced 'hot boxes' due to the overheating of axle bearings and had to be taken out of service. Furthermore, it was not uncommon to see them derail when negotiating the tight curves of the Welsh Valleys where they frequently worked. One way to minimise this was to drive the locomotive in reverse which often happened.

No. 5984. *Linden Hall.* GWR. 4-6-0. 'Class 4900' (Hall Class) locomotive. Built at Swindon in October 1938 as GWR number 5984 (later BR 5984). Withdrawn from service in January 1965 and scrapped in April 1965. (Photo P.40).

No. 6018. *King Henry VI.* GWR. 4-6-0. 'Class 6000' (King Class) locomotive. Built at Swindon in June 1928 as GWR number 6018 (later BR 6018). Withdrawn from service in December 1962 and scrapped in September 1963. (Photo P.13).

No. 6025. *King Henry III.* GWR. 4-6-0. 'Class 6000' (King Class) locomotive. Built at Swindon in July 1930 as GWR number 6025 (later BR 6025). Withdrawn from service in December 1962 and scrapped in May 1964. (Photo P.13).

No. 6026. *King John.* GWR. 4-6-0. 'Class 6000' (King Class) locomotive. Built at Swindon in July 1930 as GWR number 6026 (later BR 6026). Withdrawn from service in September 1962 and scrapped in November 1963. (Photo P.13).

'Class 6000' (King Class) - Additional information.
A total of thirty GWR 'Class 6000' (King Class) locomotives were built at Swindon between 1927 and 1930. They were designed by Charles B. Collett as express passenger locomotives (BR power classification 8P) to operate from London Paddington to Bristol, Plymouth, Cardiff, Birmingham and Wolverhampton. They were all named after British Kings.

In 1936, number 6007 *King William III* was withdrawn from service and condemned following an accident which caused extensive damage to the locomotive, rendering it uneconomical to repair. A new replacement locomotive was built, taking the overall total build of King Class locomotives to thirty-one.

Also in 1936, following the death of King George V, locomotive number 6029 *King Stephen* was renamed *King Edward VIII*, the successor to George V. Following the abdication of Edward the same year, the name of the locomotive was once again changed, to that of the new British Monarch, *King George VI.*

No.6365. GWR. 2-6-0. 'Class 4300' locomotive. Built at Swindon in October 1925 as GWR number 6365 (later BR 6365). Withdrawn from service in October 1963 and scrapped in May 1964. (Photo P.54).

'Class 4300' - Additional information.
A total of 342 'Class 4300' locomotives, designed by George Jackson Churchward for mixed traffic duties, were built between 1911 and 1932. They quickly proved themselves to be a highly efficient and successful locomotive. As well as being ideal for working goods traffic, they were ideally suited for passenger traffic, reaching speeds up to 70mph. A considerable number of these locomotives were built for

use during the First World War and eleven were shipped to France to work munitions and hospital trains during the conflict. Two members of the class have been preserved.

No. 6689. GWR. 0-6-2T. 'Class 5600' Tank locomotive. Built at Swindon in October 1928 as GWR number 6689 (later BR 6689). Withdrawn from service in June 1965 and scrapped in October 1965. (Photo P.45).

No. 6823. *Oakley Grange*. GWR. 4-6-0. 'Class 6800' (Grange Class) locomotive. Built at Swindon in January 1937 as GWR number 6823 (later BR 6823). Withdrawn from service in June 1965 and scrapped in November 1965. (Photo P.49).

No. 6835. *Eastham Grange*. GWR. 4-6-0. 'Class 6800' (Grange Class) locomotive. Built at Swindon in September 1937 as GWR number 6835 (later BR 6835). Withdrawn from service in May 1963 and scrapped in October 1963. (Photo P.62).

No. 6838. *Goodmoor Grange*. GWR. 4-6-0. 'Class 6800' (Grange Class) locomotive. Built at Swindon in September 1937 as GWR number 6838 (later BR 6838). Withdrawn from service in November 1965 and scrapped in February 1966. (Photo P.63).

No. 6873. *Caradoc Grange*. GWR. 4-6-0. 'Class 6800' (Grange Class) locomotive. Built at Swindon in April 1939 as GWR number 6873 (later BR 6873). Withdrawn from service in June 1964 and scrapped in February 1965. (Photo P.50).

'Class 6800' (Grange Class) – Additional information.
A total of eighty 'Class 6800' (Grange Class) locomotives, designed by Charles Collett, were built at Swindon between 1936 and 1939. They were designed as mixed traffic locomotives (BR 5MT) and were very similar to the GWR 'Class 4900' (Hall Class) locomotives but with smaller wheels which provided more traction.

They were originally designed to replace the 'Class 4300' mixed traffic locomotives, of which there were over 300, using their wheels and some other parts. However, only eighty of the '6800 Class' had been built when the building programme was interrupted by the events of the Second World War. After the war, plans were drawn up to nationalise the railways and the building plan for the remaining 'Class 6800' locomotives was cancelled. All eighty Grange Class locomotives were withdrawn from service between 1960 and 1965. None was preserved.

No. 6982. *Melmerby Hall*. GWR. 4-6-0. 'Class 6959' (Modified Hall Class) locomotive. Built at Swindon in January 1948 as BR 6982 (GWR design). Withdrawn from service in August 1964 and scrapped in November 1964. (Photo P.100).

'Class 6959' (Modified Hall) – Additional information.
A total of seventy-one 'Class 6959' (Modified Hall) locomotives were built at Swindon between 1944 and 1950. They were designed by Frederick Hawksworth as a development of Charles Collett's Class 4900 (Hall Class) locomotives. They were well received by crew members and maintenance staff. Although the outward appearance was basically the same as the 'Class 4900' (Hall Class), there were many significant modifications which made it a far more efficient and superior locomotive. Overall, it became a successful locomotive. Six 'Modified Hall Class' locomotives have been preserved.

No. 7001. *Sir James Milne*. GWR. 4-6-0. 'Class 4073' (Castle Class) locomotive. Built at Swindon in May 1946 as GWR number 7001 (later BR 7001). Withdrawn from service in September 1963 and scrapped in April 1964.

Number 7001 entered service on the GWR in 1946, bearing the name *Denbigh Castle*. In 1947, she was re-named *Sir James Milne*, the last General Manager of the Great Western Railway, who announced that he was retiring at the end of that year, prior to nationalisation of the railways on 1 January 1948. Sir James Milne died in 1958 at the age of seventy-four but the locomotive carried his name until it was withdrawn from service and scrapped. (Photo P.76).

No. 7815. *Fritwell Manor*. GWR. 4-6-0. 'Class 7800' (Manor Class) locomotive. Built at Swindon in January 1939 as GWR number 7815 (later BR 7815). Withdrawn from service in October 1964 and scrapped in February 1965. (Photo P.107).

'Class 7800' (Manor Class) – Additional information.
A total of twenty 'Class 7800' (Manor Class) locomotives were built at Swindon between 1938 and 1939. A further ten were produced (also at Swindon) in 1950, taking the grand total to thirty. These mixed traffic locomotives (BR power classification 5MT), were designed by Charles Collett and were a lighter version of the GWR 'Class 6800' (Grange Class), which allowed them to operate in rural districts and branch lines where heavier locomotives were prohibited from working due to weight restrictions.

Whilst the majority of 'Manor Class' locomotives could be seen working on the rural lines of Wales, including the working of the *Cambrian Coast Express*, they were successfully used in the West Country, as their weight allowed them to cross the Tamar Bridge to work on the Cornish branch lines. They were also well suited and used for carrying out banking duties on the inclines between Plymouth and Newton Abbot in South Devon.

No. 8400. GWR. 0-6-0PT. 'Class 9400' Pannier Tank locomotive. Built for BR (GWR design) by W. G. Bagnall & Co., Stafford in August 1949 as BR number 8400. Withdrawn from service in September 1964 and scrapped in December 1964. (Photo P.64).

No. 9437. GWR. 0-6-0PT. 'Class 9400' Pannier Tank locomotive. Built for BR by Robert Stephenson & Hawthorn Ltd, Darlington in January 1951 as BR number 9437. Withdrawn from service in June 1965 and scrapped in June 1965. (Photo P.65).

'Class 9400' Pannier Tank - Additional information.
A total of 210 'Class 9400' Pannier Tank locomotives were designed by Frederick Hawksworth for shunting and banking duties. Their power classification was BR 4F. The first batch of ten were built at the GWR Works in Swindon in 1947 and numbered 9400 to 9409. These were the last steam locomotives ever built by the GWR before nationalisation of the railways took place in January 1948.

After nationalisation, a further two-hundred 'Class 9400' locomotives were commissioned by British Railways and built by private contractors between 1949 and 1956. Many had very short working lives of less than ten years and number 8447 was scrapped after less than five years in service. Just two of these engines were preserved.

No. 9625. GWR. 0-6-0PT. 'Class 5700' Pannier Tank locomotive. Built at Swindon in November 1945 as GWR number 9625 (later BR 9625). Withdrawn from service in June 1965 and scrapped in October 1965. (Photo P.94).

No. 9651. GWR. 0-6-0PT. 'Class 5700' Pannier Tank locomotive. Built at Swindon in June 1946 as GWR number 9651 (later BR 9651). Withdrawn from service in July 1965 and scrapped in October 1965. (Photo P.69).

SOUTHERN RAILWAY LOCOMOTIVES
No. 30107. SR (LSWR). 0-4-4T. 'Class M7' Tank locomotive. Built at Nine Elms in April 1905 as LSWR number 107 (later BR 30107). Withdrawn from service in May 1964 and scrapped in October 1964. (Photo P.21).

'Class M7' – Additional information.
A total of 105 'Class M7' locomotives, designed by Dugald Drummond, were built for the LSWR between 1897 and 1911. These 0-4-4 tank locomotives were designed for passenger work in the busy London area of the London and South Western Railway. Their power classification was BR 2P.

The 'Class M7' locomotives were built in five separate batches, each with a number of modifications. They subsequently proved themselves to be successful suburban passenger locomotives which performed well. Some of the locomotives were fitted with push and pull apparatus and were frequently used on branch line services.

When first introduced, a number of these locomotives were used on semi-fast passenger services from London to South Coast destinations such as Plymouth, Exeter, Weymouth, Bournemouth and Southampton. All but one member of the class entered into BR stock in 1948 and sixty survived into the 1960s. 1964 saw the withdrawal of the last thirteen members of the class and just two of the locomotives, 30245 and 30053, were preserved.

No. 30313. SR (LSWR). 4-4-0. 'Class T9' locomotive. Built at Nine Elms in September 1901 as LSWR locomotive number 313. In 1923, she was absorbed into SR stock as SR number 313 (later BR 30313). Withdrawn from service in July 1961 and scrapped in September 1961. (Photo P.71).

'Class T9' – Additional information.
A total of sixty-six 'Class T9' locomotives, designed and built for the LSWR by Dugald Drummond, entered service between 1899 and 1901. They were specifically designed as express passenger locomotives and with a top speed of 85mph, they earned the nickname 'Greyhounds'. One example of the 'Class T9' locomotive (number 30120) has been preserved by the National Railway Museum in York.

No. 30541. SR. 0-6-0. 'Class Q' locomotive. Built at Eastleigh in 1939 as SR number 541 (later BR 30541). Withdrawn from service in November 1964 and subsequently preserved. She is currently owned by and based at the 'Bluebell Heritage Railway' in West Sussex. (Photo P.26).

'Class Q' – Additional information.
A total of twenty 'Class Q' freight locomotives, designed by Richard Maunsell were built between 1938 and 1939. When they were introduced into service, they

were considered to be old fashioned in design and not suitable for main line working. They were however adequate for working light and medium local goods services. Although designed for freight duties (BR power classification 4F), they were additionally fitted with a passenger carriage heating system which enabled them to work local passenger services which they occasionally did. In reality however, they were usually confined to working local freight services. 'Q Class' locomotives should not be confused with the SR 'Q1 Class' locomotives which were designed and built by Oliver Bulleid in 1942. These were more powerful and versatile locomotives than the 'Q Class' and were infinitely much more successful.

No. 30583. SR (LSWR). 4-4-2T. 'Class 0415' Tank locomotive. Built in March 1885 by Neilson and Co for the London and South Western Railway as LSWR number 488 (later SR 3488 & BR 30588). Withdrawn from service in July 1961 and subsequently preserved as a part of the Bluebell Heritage Railway in Sussex. (Photo P.21).

'Class 0415' – Additional information.
A total of seventy-one 'Class 0415' Tank locomotives, designed by William Adams, were built between 1882 and 1885, for the London and South Western Railway. Originally designed to work London suburban passenger trains (Power classification BR 1P), they were soon replaced by the more powerful Drummond 'Class M7' locomotives. Most of the class were withdrawn from service and scrapped in the 1920s and only three were left by 1928. These three were put to work on the Lyme Regis branch and continued to work the line until the 1960s.

No. 30830. SR (LSWR). 4-6-0. 'Class S15' locomotive. Built at Eastleigh in August 1927 as SR number 830 (later BR 30830). Withdrawn from service in July 1964 and subsequently bought from a scrapyard in 1987 by the Maunsell Locomotive Society for use on the Bluebell Heritage

Railway but was later re-sold to the Essex Locomotive Society who moved her to the North Yorkshire Moors Railway. As of 2020, the locomotive was still in storage at an undisclosed location, hopefully still destined to be restored as a working locomotive sometime in the future. (Photo P.106).

No. 30832. SR (LSWR). 4-6-0. 'Class S15' locomotive. Built at Eastleigh in October 1927 as SR number 832 (later BR 30832). Withdrawn from service in January 1964 and scrapped in February 1964. (Photo P.105).

'Class S15' – Additional information. A total of forty-five 'Class S15' locomotives, designed for the LSWR by Robert Urie, were built at Eastleigh between 1920 and 1936. These locomotives were reliable and frequently used to work heavy goods express services between Southampton and Nine Elms Goods Depot in London (Power Classification BR 6F). All were withdrawn from service between 1962 and 1966.

No. 30860. *Lord Hawke.* SR. 4-6-0. 'Class LN' (Lord Nelson Class) locomotive. Built at Nine Elms in April 1929 as SR number 860 (later BR 30860). Withdrawn from service in August 1962 and scrapped in August 1962. (Photo P.91).

'Class LN' (Lord Nelson Class) – Additional information. Just sixteen 'Lord Nelson Class' locomotives, designed by Richard Maunsell, were built at Eastleigh Works between 1926 and 1929. They were initially designed as passenger locomotives (power classification 7P), to work boat trains between London Victoria and Dover. Later they were used on express passenger services to other south coast resorts. The locomotives were all named after famous British Royal Navy Admirals and the first member of the class, number 30850 *Lord Nelson,* has been preserved as a part of the National Collection by the National Railway Museum in York but is currently on loan to the Mid Hants Heritage Railway.

No. 30925. *Cheltenham.* SR. 4-4-0. 'Class V' (Schools Class) locomotive. Built at Eastleigh in July 1934 as SR number 925 (later BR 30925). Withdrawn from service in December 1962 and subsequently preserved as a part of the National Collection, owned by the National Railway Museum in York. (Photo P.33).

No. 30935. *Sevenoaks.* SR. 4-4-0. 'Class V' (Schools Class) locomotive. Built at Eastleigh in June 1935 as SR number 935 (later BR 30935). Withdrawn from service in December 1962 and scrapped in May 1964. (Photo P.34).

'Class V' (Schools Class) – Additional information. A total of forty 'Class V' (Schools Class) locomotives, designed by Richard Maunsell, were built at Eastleigh between 1930 and 1935. They were a smaller version of the 'Lord Nelson Class' (LN Class) locomotives but with certain modifications. They were also the most powerful 4-4-0 locomotive ever produced in Britain (BR power classification 5P).

'Class V' locomotives were all named after English public schools and were more commonly referred to as 'Schools Class' locomotives. They were built to haul intermediate express and semi-fast passenger trains and were capable of speeds in excess of 90mph. Three examples of the class have been preserved.

No. 31802. SR. 2-6-0. 'Class U' locomotive. Built at Ashford in July 1928 as SR number 1802 (later BR 31802). Withdrawn from service in September 1964 and scrapped in December 1964. (Photo P.52).

'Class U' – Additional information. A total of fifty 'Class U' locomotives (nicknamed 'U Boats') were produced at Ashford, Brighton and Eastleigh between 1928 and 1931. Designed by Richard Maunsell as mixed traffic locomotives (BR power classification 4P3F). The first twenty members of the class, numbers 31790 to 31809, were rebuilds of former

South East and Chatham 2-6-4T, 'K Class' (River Class), tank locomotives. Number 31802 (see page 52) was rebuilt from SEC 'K Class' (River Class) tank locomotive number 802 *River Cuckmere*. A total of four 'Class U' locomotives have been preserved.

No. 31873. SR (SEC). 2-6-0 'Class N' locomotive. Built at Ashford in September 1925 as SR number 1873 (later BR 31873). Withdrawn from service in January 1966 and scrapped in April 1966. (Photo P.92).

'Class N' – Additional information.
A total of eighty 'Class N' locomotives were built at Ashford Works for the South East and Chatham Railway, between 1917 and 1934. Designed by Richard Maunsell, over half of these engines were assembled from parts produced at the Royal Arsenal in Woolwich, giving rise to the nickname 'Woolworths Locomotives'. They were designed to be used as mixed traffic locomotives (BR power classification 4MT, later re-classified as 4P5F).

No. 32646. SR (LBSCR). 0-6-0T. 'Class A1X' Tank locomotive. Built at Brighton for the LBSCR in December 1876 as LBSCR number 46 (later LBSCR 646, SR number W2 and BR 32646). 32646 was sold to the LSWR as number 734 in March 1903 to work the Lyme Regis branch line where she remained until being shipped to the Isle of Wight in 1913, on loan to the Freshwater, Yarmouth and Newport Railway who later purchased her.

After the 1923 railway groupings, she was taken into the stock of the SR but continued working on the Isle of Wight as number W2 and given the name *Freshwater*, after a village on the Island. She was later re-numbered W8.

32646 was transferred back to the mainland after nationalisation took place in 1948 and she worked the Hayling Island branch line until being withdrawn from service in November 1963. During her BR service she was nicknamed *Hayling Billy*, together with other locomotives working the Hayling branch line services. After

being withdrawn from BR service, she was purchased for preservation by the Sadler Railcar Company and after undergoing changes of ownership, she was eventually donated to the Isle of Wight Steam Heritage Railway where she continues to work. (Photo P.70).

'Class A1X' (Former Class A1) – Additional information.
A total of fifty 'Class A1' Tank locomotives were built at Brighton by the LBSCR between 1872 and 1880. They were given nicknames 'rooters' and 'terriers'. They were designed by William Stroudley and built as passenger locomotives to work London Suburban trains out of London Bridge and Victoria stations. Due to the rapid increase in passengers at the time, these locomotives (BR classification 0P), were quickly replaced by more powerful engines and they were transferred to other duties, with the majority being put to work on branch line services. After 1911, seventeen members of the class (including 32646) were rebuilt as 'Class A1X' locomotives.

No. 33020. SR. 0-6-0. 'Class Q1' locomotive. Built at Ashford in May 1942 as SR number C20 (later BR 33020). Withdrawn from service in January 1966 and scrapped in August 1966. (Photo P.53).

No. 33039. SR. 0-6-0. 'Class Q1' locomotive. Built at Brighton in December 1942 as SR number C39 (later BR 33039). Withdrawn from service in June 1964 and scrapped in December 1964. (Photo P.101).

'Class Q1' – Additional information.
A total of forty 'Class Q1' Austerity locomotives, designed by Oliver Bulleid, were built at Brighton and Ashford (twenty each) in 1942 in response to the need for powerful freight locomotives to transport the vast amount of wartime freight and munitions through Southern England destined for Mainland Europe. Due to their controversial shape and design, they were given nicknames such as 'Ugly Ducklings',

'Coffee Pots' and 'Charlies'. With a power classification of BR 5F, they were the most powerful 0-6-0 locomotives ever built in Britain. One example is preserved at the National Railway Museum in York.

No. 34001. *Exeter*. SR. 4-6-2. 'Class WC' (West Country Class) locomotive. Built at Brighton in June 1945 as SR number 21C101 (later BR 34001). Withdrawn from service in July 1967 and scrapped in October 1967. (Photo P.69).

No. 34006. *Bude*. SR. 4-6-2. 'Class WC' (West Country Class) locomotive. Built at Brighton in July 1945 as SR number 21C106 (later BR 34006). Withdrawn from service in March 1967 and scrapped in October 1967. (Photo P.30).

No. 34021. *Dartmoor*. SR. 4-6-2. 'Class WC' (West Country Class) locomotive. Built at Brighton in January 1946 as SR number 21C121 (later BR 34021). Withdrawn from service in July 1967 and scrapped in March 1968. (Photos P.29/30).

No. 34028. *Eddystone*. SR. 4-6-2. 'Class WC' (Rebuilt West Country Class) locomotive. Built at Brighton in April 1946 as SR number 21C128 (later BR 34028). Withdrawn from service in May 1964. She was subsequently preserved and is owned by Southern Locomotives Ltd and operates on the Swanage Heritage Railway in Dorset. (Photo P.56).

No. 34031. *Torrington*. SR. 4-6-2. 'Class WC' (West Country Class) locomotive. Built at Brighton in June 1946 as SR number 21C131 (later BR 34031). Withdrawn from service in February 1965 and scrapped in May 1965. (Photo P.14).

No. 34054. *Lord Beaverbrook*. SR. 4-6-2. 'Class BB' (Battle of Britain Class) locomotive. Built at Brighton in February 1947 as SR number 21C154 (later BR 34054). Withdrawn from service in September 1964 and scrapped in March 1965. (Photo P.14).

No. 34072. *257 Squadron*. SR. 4-6-2. 'Class BB' (Battle of Britain Class) locomotive. Built at Brighton in April 1948 as BR 34072. Withdrawn from service in October 1964 but was subsequently bought for preservation by Southern Locomotives Limited. Currently preserved, fully operational and working on the Swanage Heritage Railway in Dorset. (Photo P.31).

No. 34077. *603 Squadron*. SR. 4-6-2. 'Class BB' (Battle of Britain Class) locomotive. Built at Brighton for BR in July 1948 as BR number 34077. Withdrawn from service in March 1967 and scrapped in August 1967. (Photo P.15).

No. 34085. *501 Squadron*. SR. 4-6-2. 'Class BB' (Battle of Britain Class) locomotive. Built at Brighton for BR in November 1948 as BR number 34085. Withdrawn from service in September 1965 and scrapped in April 1966. (Photo P.55).

No. 34087. *145 Squadron*. SR. 4-6-2. 'Class BB' (Battle of Britain Class) locomotive. Built at Brighton for BR in December 1948 as BR number 34087. Withdrawn from service in July 1967 and scrapped in September 1968. (Photo P.80).

No. 34088. *213 Squadron*. SR. 4-6-2. 'Class BB' (Battle of Britain Class) locomotive. Built at Brighton for BR in December 1948 as BR number 34088. Withdrawn from service in March 1967 and scrapped in March 1968. (Photo P.68).

No. 34089. *602 Squadron*. SR. 4-6-2. 'Class BB' (Battle of Britain Class) locomotive. Built at Brighton for BR in December 1948 as BR number 34089. Withdrawn from service in July 1967 and scrapped in September 1968. (Photo P.41).

No. 34106. *Lydford*. SR. 4-6-2. 'Class WC' (West Country Class) locomotive. Built at Brighton for BR in March 1950 as BR number 34106. Withdrawn from service in October 1964 and scrapped in December 1964. (Photo P.80).

'Class WC & BB' (West Country Class & Battle of Britain Class) – Additional information. A total of 110 'WC Class' (West Country Class) and 'BB Class' (Battle of Britain

Class) locomotives were built at Brighton and Eastleigh Works between 1945 and 1951. Designed by Oliver Bulleid, these two classes of Light Pacific locomotives (nicknamed Spam Cans) were identical in design apart from the type of name which they were allocated.

'WC Class' locomotives were named after resorts in the West Country, served by the former Southern Railway Company, and were normally confined to working in those areas. 'BB Class' locomotives were named after people, places and events surrounding the Royal Air Force and Battle of Britain which took place in 1940. 'BB Class' locomotives were generally based in the South-East of England, operating in the areas most associated with the Battle of Britain. A total of sixty 'WC Class' and 'BB Class' were rebuilt between 1955 and 1961.

No. 35004. *Cunard White Star*. SR. 4-6-2. 'Class MN' (Merchant Navy Class) locomotive. Built at Eastleigh in December 1941 as SR number 21C4 (later BR 35004). Withdrawn from service in October 1965 and scrapped in January 1966. (Photo P.40).

No. 35012. *United States Line*. SR. 4-6-2. 'Class MN' (Merchant Navy Class) locomotive. Built at Eastleigh in January 1945 as SR number 21C12 (later BR 35012). Withdrawn from service in April 1967 and scrapped in September 1968. (Photos P.26 and P.64).

No. 35014. *Nederland Line*. SR. 4-6-2. 'Class MN' (Merchant Navy Class) locomotive. Built at Eastleigh in February 1945 as SR number 21C14 (later BR 35014). Withdrawn from service in March 1967 and scrapped in September 1967. (Photo P.81).

No. 35019. *French Line CGT*. SR. 4-6-2. 'Class MN' (Merchant Navy Class) locomotive. Built at Eastleigh in June 1945 as SR number 21C19 (later BR 35019). Withdrawn from service in September 1965 and scrapped in February 1966. (Photo P.15).

No. 35023. *Holland-Afrika Line*. SR. 4-6-2. 'Class MN' (Merchant Navy Class)

locomotive. Built at Eastleigh for BR in November 1948 as BR number 35023. Withdrawn from service in July 1967 and scrapped in April 1968. (Photo P.63).

'MN Class' (Merchant Navy Class) – Additional Information.

A total of thirty 'Class MN' (Merchant Navy Class) locomotives were built at Eastleigh between 1941 and 1949. Designed by Oliver Bulleid, these Pacific locomotives (together with 'BB Class' & 'WC Class') were commonly referred to as 'spam cans' or 'packets'. 'MN Class' locomotives were all named after Merchant Navy shipping lines which used Southampton Docks which were formerly owned by the Southern Railway Company.

'Merchant Navy Class' locomotives were extremely powerful (BR 8P), capable of reaching speeds in excess of 100 mph. They were specifically designed to haul express passenger trains on the South Western Main Line from London Waterloo to Southampton and Bournemouth. Originally built with air-smoothed casing, the whole class were later rebuilt (after 1955) and the casing was removed. Eleven members of the class were preserved.

No. W24. *Calbourne*. SR (LSWR). 0-4-4T. 'Class 02' Tank locomotive. Built for the LSWR at Nine Elms in December 1891 as LSWR number 209. Absorbed into SR stock in 1923 and transferred to the Isle of Wight in 1925 as SR (IOW) number W24 and given the name *Calbourne* after a village on the island. Withdrawn from service in March 1967 and subsequently preserved. Currently operates on the Isle of Wight Steam Railway. (Photo P.94).

No. W29. *Alverstone*. SR. (LSWR). 0-4-4T. 'Class 02' Tank locomotive. Built for the LSWR at Nine Elms in August 1891 as LSWR number 202. Absorbed into SR stock in 1923 and transferred to the Isle of Wight in 1926 as SR (IOW) number W29 and given the name *Alverstone* after a village on the island. Withdrawn from service in May 1966 and scrapped in May 1967. (Photo P.22).

No. W30. *Shorwell*. SR. (LSWR). 0-4-4T. 'Class 02' Tank locomotive. Built for the LSWR at Nine Elms in September 1892 as LSWR number 219. Absorbed into SR stock in 1923 and transferred to the Isle of Wight in 1926 as SR (IOW) number W30 and given the name *Shorwell* after a village on the island. Withdrawn from service in September 1965 and scrapped in November 1967. (Photo P.95).

'Class 02' - Additional information.
A total of sixty 'Class 02' Tank locomotives, designed by William Adams, were built at Nine Elms for the LSWR between 1889 and 1896. These 0-4-4 Tank engines were designed to work the rapidly increasing number of commuter trains in and out of London during the 1880s. The numbers of commuters continued to rise and by the turn of the century the 'Class 02' locomotives (BR power classification 0P) were no longer suitable for their original purpose and were replaced by more powerful locomotives. Consequently, 'Class 02' locomotives were dispersed to other parts of the network to work lighter passenger services. They were ideally suited for working on branch lines. All sixty locomotives were absorbed into the Southern Railway in 1923 where they worked for a further decade before any withdrawals took place. Forty-eight survived into the 1950s.

'Class 02' locomotives are mainly associated with the Isle of Wight. Many families have fond memories of these little engines standing on Ryde Pier to greet passengers alighting from the ferries or transporting the many thousands of holidaymakers around the Island. The first two 'Class 02' locomotives were shipped across the Solent to the Isle of Wight shortly after the railway groupings in 1923. They became an instant success. Further '02' locomotives continued to be transported there until the numbers reached twenty-three by 1950. The locomotives were later re-numbered from fourteen to thirty-six preceded by the letter 'W'. Each of the locomotives were also

'named' after a resort, village or place on the Island. Of the twenty-three 'Class 02' locomotives on the Isle of Wight in 1950, four were withdrawn from service during 1955 and 1956. The remaining nineteen were withdrawn between 1962 and 1967. Only one, number W24 *Calbourne*, has been preserved and can still be seen working on the Isle of Wight Steam Heritage Railway.

LONDON MIDLAND AND SCOTTISH RAILWAY LOCOMOTIVES.

No. 40646. LMS. 4-4-0. 'Class 2P' locomotive. Built at Crewe in September 1931 as LMS number 646 (later BR 40646). Withdrawn from service in May 1962 and scrapped in September 1962. (Photo P.33).

Class 2P – Additional information.
A total of 138 of these 4-4-0 locomotives, designed by Henry Fowler, were built at Crewe and Derby between 1928 and 1932. They were designed and built for light passenger work (power classification BR 2P).

Locomotive numbers LMS 591 and 639 were withdrawn from service and scrapped in 1933, after being extensively damaged in an accident at Glasgow. The remaining 136 engines became part of the stock of BR locomotives in 1948 and with the exception of two, they all survived until the end of the 1950s. They were withdrawn from service between 1959 and 1962.

No. 41204. LMS. 2-6-2T. 'Class 2MT' Tank locomotive. Built at Crewe in December 1946 as LMS number 1204 (later BR 41204). Withdrawn from service in December 1966 and scrapped in April 1967. (Photo P.23).

'Class 2MT' – Additional information.
A total of 130 of these 2-6-2 tank locomotives, designed by H.G. Ivatt, were built at Crewe and Derby between 1946 and 1952. They were designed for light passenger work and given an LMS power classification 2P. When the engines were taken into BR stock it was decided to use them as mixed traffic locomotives and they were re-classified as BR power classification 2MT. Due to their size, they were given the

nickname 'Mickey Mouse'. The locomotive design formed the basis of the 'Standard Class 2', 2-6-2 tank locomotive which was later produced by BR.

No. 41533. LMS (MR). 'Class 0F' (zero F).0-4-0T. Former 'Class 1928' Tank locomotive. Built for the MR at Derby in July 1921 as MR number 1533. Absorbed into LMS stock in 1923 as LMS number 1533 (later BR 41533). Mothballed in October 1965 until being officially withdrawn from service in December 1966. Scrapped in April 1967. (Photo P.107).

'Class 0F' (zero F). Former 'MR Class 1928', 'BR Class 0F (zero F)' – Additional information.
Just five of these small 0-4-0 shunting engines, designed by Richard Deeley, were originally built for the Midland Railway in 1907 as MR 'Class 1928' locomotives. Some fourteen years later, a further five were built in 1921/1922, taking the total to ten. All were fitted with 'stove pipe' chimneys. These tiny locomotives were built exclusively to work in such places as docks, yards, industrial premises and places where sharp curves were to be found. After they were absorbed into the LMS Railway Company in 1923, they were de-classified and remained as un-classed engines. After 1948, BR classified the locomotives under their power classification 0F (zero F). All were withdrawn from service between 1957 and 1966.

No. 41835. LMS (MR). 0-6-0T. 'Class 1F' Tank locomotive. Built for the MR by the Vulcan Foundry, Lancashire in October 1892 as MR number 1835. Absorbed into LMS stock in 1923 as LMS number 1835 (Later BR 41835). Withdrawn from service in December 1966 and scrapped in April 1967. (Photo P.23).

'Class 1F' – Additional information.
A total of 240 of these Johnson design tank locomotives were built for the MR both at Derby and by outside contractors between 1875 and 1908. They were successfully used as shunting locomotives all over the network. Some had open back or half cabs whilst others were fitted with enclosed cabs. Over half of these locomotives were rebuilt after 1918.

No. 44082. LMS. 0-6-0. 'Class 4F' locomotive. Built in September 1925 by Kerr, Stuart & Co. at Stoke-on-Trent as LMS 4082 (later BR 44082). Withdrawn from service in August 1961 and scrapped in September 1961. (Photo P.28).

No. 44137. LMS. 0-6-0. 'Class 4F' locomotive. Built at Crewe in October 1925 for the LMS as LMS number 4137 (later BR 44137). Withdrawn from service in February 1965 and scrapped in November 1965. (Photo P.74).

No. 44212. LMS. 0-6-0. 'Class 4F' locomotive. Built at Derby in December 1925 for the LMS as LMS number 4212 (later BR 44212). Withdrawn from service in December 1963 and scrapped in May 1964. (Photo P.29).

No. 44265. LMS. 0-6-0. 'Class 4F' locomotive. Built at Derby in October 1926 for the LMS as LMS number 4265 (later BR 44265). Withdrawn from service in December 1963 and scrapped in May 1964. (Photo P.73).

No. 44411. LMS. 0-6-0. 'Class 4F' locomotive. Built at Derby in September 1927 for the LMS as LMS number 4411 (later BR 44411). Withdrawn from service in October 1963 and scrapped in April 1964. (Photo P.28).

'Class 4F'. 'Duck Sixes' – Additional information.
A total of 575 of these locomotives, designed by Henry Fowler, were built between 1924 and 1941. The locomotive design was based upon Fowler's earlier Midland Railway 'Class 3835' which was introduced in 1911, and was very similar in design, apart from having a left-hand drive as opposed to a right-hand drive.

The 'Class 4F' was designed and built as a standard goods locomotive to work medium freight traffic and they earned the nickname 'Duck Sixes' due to their 0-6-0 wheel arrangement. Unfortunately, the 'Duck Sixes' frequently suffered mechanical failures due to 'hot axle boxes' caused by overheating of the bearings. However, this problem was later overcome by the installation of mechanical lubricators, after which they became successful and reliable locomotives. Although designed for freight duties, in later years it was not uncommon to see them working local passenger services.

No. 44830. LMS. 4-6-0. 'Class 5' (Black Five) locomotive. Built at Crewe in August 1944 for the LMS as LMS number 4830 (later BR 44830). Withdrawn from service in August 1967 and scrapped in January 1968. (Photo P.85).

No. 45104. LMS. 4-6-0. 'Class 5' (Black Five) locomotive. Built for the LMS by the Vulcan Foundry in Lancashire in May 1945 as LMS number 5104 (later BR 45104). Withdrawn from service in June 1968 and scrapped in October 1968. (Photo P.105).

No. 45211. LMS. 4-6-0. 'Class 5' (Black Five) locomotive. Built for the LMS by Armstrong Whitworth, Locomotive Works, Newcastle in November 1935 as LMS number 5211 (later BR 45211). Withdrawn from service in May 1967 and scrapped in October 1967. (Photo P.86).

No. 45258. LMS. 4-6-0. 'Class 5' (Black Five) locomotive. Built for the LMS by Armstrong Whitworth, Locomotive Works, Newcastle in October 1936 as LMS number 5258 (later BR 45258). Withdrawn from service in March 1968 and scrapped in June 1968. (Photo P.97).

No. 45290. LMS. 4-6-0. 'Class 5' (Black Five) locomotive. Built for the LMS by Armstrong Whitworth, Locomotive Works, Newcastle in December 1936 as LMS number 5290 (later BR 45290). Withdrawn from service in June 1968 and scrapped in October 1968. (Photo P.96).

No. 45495. LMS. 4-6-0. 'Class 5' (Black Five) locomotive. Built at Derby in February 1944 for the LMS as LMS number 5495 (later BR 45495). Withdrawn from service in March 1967 and scrapped in March 1967. (Photo P.104).

'Class 5' (Black Five) – Additional information.
A total of 842 LMS 'Class 5' (Black Five) mixed traffic locomotives, designed by William Stanier, were built between 1934 and 1951. Shortly after being introduced into service, they became known as 'Black Staniers' due to being painted black as opposed to the red livery used on the Stanier 4-6-0 'Jubilee Class' locomotives which were being built at the same time. Later they became known as 'Black Fives' after the LMS power classification of 5P5F which was painted on both sides of the cab.

Black Five locomotives were designed as an all-purpose mixed traffic locomotive and were the LMS equivalent of the highly successful GWR '4900 Class' (Hall Class) locomotives. The 'Black Fives' turned out to be the most reliable and efficient design of general purpose locomotive ever built in Britain. They were extremely popular amongst the drivers and were used all over the country. Withdrawals of the 'Class 5' locomotives from service took place between 1961 and 1968 and they were amongst the last steam locomotives to operate on the railway network before steam was replaced by diesel and electric traction. The power classification of the 'Class 5' was changed from 5P5F to 5MT by BR after nationalisation of the railways took place. A total of eighteen 'Black Fives' have been preserved.

No. 45504. *Royal Signals*. LMS. 4-6-0. 'Patriot Class' locomotive. Built at Crewe in July 1932 as LMS number 5504 (later BR 45504). Withdrawn from service in March 1962 and scrapped in March 1962. (Photo P.92).

No. 45505. *The Royal Army Ordnance Corps*. LMS. 4-6-0. 'Patriot Class' locomotive. Built at Crewe in July 1932 as LMS number 5505 (later BR 45505). Withdrawn from service in June 1962 and scrapped in August 1962. (Photo P.17).

No. 45506. *The Royal Pioneer Corps*. LMS. 4-6-0. 'Patriot Class' locomotive. Built at Crewe in August 1932 as LMS number 5506 (later BR 45506). Withdrawn from service in March 1962 and scrapped in March 1962. (Photo P.78).

'Patriot Class' – Additional information. A total of fifty-two 'Patriot Class' locomotives, designed by Sir Henry Fowler and sometimes referred to as 'Baby Scots', were built at Crewe (42) and Derby (10) between 1930 and 1934. They were designed for use as express passenger locomotives with a power classification of 5XP, a classification between 5P and 6P. After nationalisation, BR utilized the locomotives for mixed traffic duties and they were re-classified as 6P5F in 1951. A total of eighteen 'Patriot Class' locomotives were rebuilt between 1946 and 1949 to create a new class of locomotive called the LMS 'Rebuilt Patriot Class'. The remaining thirty-four 'Patriot Class' locomotives which were not rebuilt, were all withdrawn from service between 1960 and 1962. None was preserved.

No. 45564. *New South Wales*. LMS. 4-6-0. 'Jubilee Class' locomotive. Built for the LMS by the North British Locomotive Company, Glasgow in August 1934 as LMS number 5564 (later BR 45564). Withdrawn from service in July 1964 and scrapped in December 1964. (Photo P.42).

No. 45570. *New Zealand*. LMS. 4-6-0. 'Jubilee Class' locomotive. Built for the LMS by the North British Locomotive Company, Glasgow in August 1934 as LMS number 5570 (later BR 45570). Withdrawn from service in December 1962 and scrapped in July 1963. (Photo P.82).

No. 45596. *Bahamas*. LMS. 4-6-0. 'Jubilee Class' locomotive. Built for the LMS by the North British Locomotive Company, Glasgow in January 1935 as LMS number 5596 (later BR 45596). Withdrawn from service in July 1966 and subsequently preserved. 45596 is currently owned by the 'Bahamas Locomotive Society' and based

at Ingrow West on the Keighley & Worth Valley Heritage Railway. (Photo P.83).

No. 45648. *Wemyss*. LMS. 4-6-0. 'Jubilee Class' locomotive. Built at Crewe in January 1935 as LMS number 5648 (later BR 45648). Withdrawn from service in February 1963 and scrapped in March 1963. (Photo P.50).

'Jubilee Class' – Additional information. A total of 191 'Jubilee Class' locomotives, designed by William Stanier, were built between 1934 and 1936. The locomotives were named 'Jubilee Class' locomotives to commemorate the Silver Jubilee of George V, which took place in May 1935. The first member of the class, number 5552 (later BR 45552) which was built in June 1934, was allocated the name *Silver Jubilee* in April 1935.

The 'Jubilee Class' locomotives were built at Crewe (131), Derby (10) and the North British Works in Glasgow (50) for use as express passenger locomotives. After being built, they left the workshops painted in 'crimson lake' red livery. Their power classification was originally LMS 5XP, a power classification between 5P and 6P. They were later re-classified by BR to 6P in 1951 and revised to 6P5F in November 1955 when they started to be used as mixed traffic locomotives.

One member of the class, number 45637 *Windward Isles*, was scrapped in 1952 following an accident. The remainder were withdrawn from service between 1960 and 1967. Four members of the class have been preserved.

No. 45735. *Comet*. LMS. 4-6-0. 'Rebuilt Jubilee Class' locomotive. Built at Crewe in November 1936 as LMS number 5735 (later BR 45735). Withdrawn from service in September 1964 and scrapped in January 1965. (Rebuilt in May 1942.). (Photo P.86).

No. 45736. *Phoenix*. LMS. 4-6-0. 'Rebuilt Jubilee Class' locomotive. Built at Crewe in November 1936 as LMS 5736 (later BR 45736). Withdrawn from service in September 1964 and scrapped in January 1965. (Rebuilt in April 1942.). (Photo P.87).

'Rebuilt Jubilee Class' – Additional information.

45735 *Comet*, together with sister locomotive 45736, *Phoenix*, were the only two 'Jubilee Class' locomotives to be rebuilt. They were both rebuilt in 1942 with 'Type 2A Taper Boilers' (originally 'Type 3A' boilers) and both were fitted with double chimneys. Their power classification was up-graded from LMS 5XP to LMS 6P (later re-classified as BR 7P). Both locomotives were withdrawn from service in September 1964 and scrapped in January 1965.

Originally it was decided that all 191 'Jubilee Class' locomotives would be rebuilt and the rebuilds commenced with LMS number 5736, *Phoenix*, being rebuilt in April 1942 and LMS number 5735, *Comet*, being rebuilt in May 1942. The rebuilding programme was then put on hold for review, following the events surrounding the Second World War which was taking place at the time.

A decision was later reached that the 'Royal Scot Class' locomotives, of which there were seventy, would be rebuilt because their boilers and cylinders, which were over ten years old and 'life expired', were already in need of replacement.

On the other hand, the boilers which had been removed from the two rebuilt 'Jubilee Class' locomotives were in good condition and had been refurbished for re-use. Consequently, the seventy 'Royal Scot' locomotives were subsequently rebuilt and in 1943, the rebuilding programme for the 'Jubilee Class' locomotives was cancelled. The remaining 189 un-rebuilt Jubilee locomotives were never rebuilt.

No. 45737. *Atlas*. LMS. 4-6-0. 'Jubilee Class' locomotive. Built at Crewe in November 1936 as LMS 5737 (later BR 45737). Withdrawn from service in May 1964 and scrapped in November 1964. (Photo P.16).

No. 46109. *Royal Engineer*. LMS. 4-6-0. 'Royal Scot Class' locomotive. Built for the LMS by the North British Locomotive Company, Glasgow in September 1927 as LMS number 6109 (later BR 46109). Withdrawn from service in December 1962 and scrapped in December 1963. (Photo P.79).

No. 46130. *The West Yorkshire Regiment*. LMS. 4-6-0. 'Royal Scot Class' locomotive. Built for the LMS by the North British Locomotive Company, Glasgow in August 1927 as LMS number 6130 (later BR 46130). Withdrawn from service in December 1962 and scrapped in October 1963. (Photo P.17).

No. 46147. *The Northamptonshire Regiment*. LMS. 4-6-0. 'Royal Scot Class' locomotive. Built for the LMS by the North British Locomotive Company, Glasgow in October 1927 as LMS number 6147 (later BR 46147). Withdrawn from service in November 1962 and scrapped in March 1963. (Photo P.96).

No. 46148. *The Manchester Regiment*. LMS 4-6-0. 'Royal Scot Class' locomotive. Built for the LMS by the North British Locomotive Company, Glasgow in December 1927 as LMS number 6148 (later BR 46148). Withdrawn from service in November 1964 and scrapped in January 1965. (Photo P.93).

'Royal Scot Class' – Additional information.

A total of seventy 'Royal Scot Class' locomotives were built between 1927 and 1930 at the North British Locomotive Works in Glasgow (50) and the LMS Works at Crewe (20). These powerful locomotives (6P), designed by Sir Henry Fowler, were built to haul express passenger trains on the West Coast Main Line.

All seventy of these locomotives were later rebuilt to a design by William Stanier and re-classified as 7P locomotives. Numbers 46100, *Royal Scot*, and 46115, *Scots Guardsman*, are the only two 'Royal Scot Class' locomotives in preservation, the remainder were scrapped.

No. 46206. *Princess Marie Louise*. LMS. 4-6-2. 'Princess Royal Class' locomotive. Built at Crewe in August 1935 as LMS number 6206 (later BR 46206). Withdrawn from service in October 1962 and scrapped in November 1962. (Photo P.16).

'Princess Royal Class' – Additional information.
Just twelve 'Princess Royal Class' locomotives were designed and built by William Stanier. The first two were built in 1933 and a further ten were built in 1935. They were powerful (7P) express passenger locomotives designed specifically to operate on the West Coast Main Line between London and Glasgow. In 1951, the 'Princess Royal Class' locomotives were re-classified as BR 8P locomotives. They were all named after a Royal Princess and number 6201, *Princess Elizabeth*, together with number 6203, *Princess Margaret Rose,* have been preserved. The remainder were scrapped.

No. 47295. LMS. 0-6-0T. 'Class 3F' (Fowler Jinty) tank locomotive. Built in October 1924 by the Hunslet Engineering Company in Leeds as LMS 7295 (later BR 47295). Withdrawn from service in April 1965 and scrapped in July 1965. (Photo P.42).

No. 47325. LMS. 0-6-0T. 'Class 3F' (Fowler Jinty) tank locomotive. Built in June 1926 by the North British Locomotive Company, Glasgow as LMS number 7325 (later BR 47325). Withdrawn from service in September 1965 and scrapped in June 1966. (Photo P.57).

No. 47631. LMS. 0-6-0T. 'Class 3F' (Fowler Jinty) tank locomotive. Built in December 1928 by William Beardmore & Co, Engineering Works, Glasgow as LMS number 7631 (later BR 47631). Withdrawn from service in June 1966 and scrapped in February 1967. (Photo P.41).

No. 47667. LMS. 0-6-0T. 'Class 3F' (Fowler Jinty) tank locomotive. Built in April 1931 at the Horwich Locomotive Works in Bolton, Lancashire, as LMS number 7667 (later BR 47667). Withdrawn from service in November 1966 and scrapped in February 1967. (Photo P.58).

'Class 3F' – Additional Information.
A total of 422 'Class 3F' Tank locomotives, designed by Henry Fowler, were built for the LMS between 1924 and 1931, plus an additional seven which were built for use on the Somerset and Dorset Joint Railway. They quickly earned the nickname 'Jinty Tank Engines' or 'Jinties'. They were a development of Samuel Johnson's rebuilt former Midland Railway '2441 Class' locomotives. With a power classification of 3F, they were useful and versatile little engines, ideal for shunting and pilot duties. They were also used as banking engines, departmental locomotives and even used on some local passenger services. A few were later used to operate push and pull passenger trains on the Western Region of BR.

No. 48310. LMS. 2-8-0. 'Class 8F' locomotive. Built at Crewe in December 1943 as LMS number 8310 (later BR 48310). Withdrawn from service in December 1967 and scrapped in May 1968. (Photo P.95).

'Class 8F' – Additional information.
A total of 852 'Class 8F' heavy freight locomotives, designed by William Stanier, were built between 1935 and 1946 and turned out to be extremely efficient and successful locomotives. A considerable number of these locomotives were commissioned by the War Department and a number were shipped abroad for use during the Second World War until 1943 when the 2-8-0 WD Austerity locomotives were introduced as a cheaper alternative.

No. 49618. LMS. 0-8-0. 'Class 7F' (Fowler) locomotive. Built at Crewe in April 1931 as LMS 9618 (later BR 49618). Withdrawn from service in October 1961 and scrapped in November 1962. (Photo P.35).

'Class 7F' – Additional information.
A total of 175, 0-8-0, 'Class 7F' locomotives, designed by Sir Henry Fowler, were built between 1929 and 1932. They were nicknamed 'Baby Austin's' or 'Austin 7s', after the then popular Austin motor car.

A development of the LNWR 'Class G2' locomotives, these engines were economical and powerful but were unfortunately prone to problems with the wheel bearings and lubrication which resulted in 'hot axle boxes' which necessitated the locomotives being taken out of service.

No. 51244. LMS (LYR). 0-4-0ST. 'Class 0F (zero F), Pug' Saddle Tank locomotive. Built at Horwich Works, Bolton in May 1910 for the Lancashire and Yorkshire Railway Company as LYR 'Class 21', number 28 (later became LMS number 11244 & BR 51244). Withdrawn from service in March 1962 and scrapped in April 1962. (Photo P.108).

'Class 0F' (zero F) - Former LYR 'Class 21' – Additional information.
Three LYR 0-6-0 'Class 21' Saddle Tank locomotives, designed by John Aspinall, were initially built by the Vulcan Foundry at Newton-le-Willows, Lancashire in 1886. A further fifty-seven, with a modified design, were later built at the Horwich Locomotive Works in Bolton between 1891 and 1910. They were given the name 'Pug' locomotives and were designed to be used as dock shunting engines.

No. 52121. LMS (LYR) 0-6-0. 'Class 27' locomotive. Built at Horwich Works, Bolton as 'Class LYR 27', number 1081 (later became LMS number 12121 & BR 52121). Withdrawn from service in November 1962 and scrapped in December 1962. (Photo P.19).

'Class 3F' (LMS & BR) Former LYR 'Class 27' – Additional information.
A total of 484 LYR 'Class 27' locomotives (also known as 'Class F19s'), were built between 1889 and 1918. Designed by John Aspinall as standard goods engines for the Lancashire & Yorkshire Railway Company, with a BR power classification of 3F. More 'Class 27' locomotives were built for the LYR than any other class of locomotives. Some were later rebuilt.

246 of these locomotives survived into the BR era and sixty were still working in the 1960s.

No. 53804. LMS (SDJR). 2-8-0. 'Class 7F' locomotive. Built at Derby for the SDJR in April 1914 as SDJR number 84 (later LMS 13804 & BR 53804). Withdrawn from service in February 1962 and scrapped in February 1962. (Photo P.34).

'Class 7F' LMS (SDJR) – Additional information.
Eleven 'Class 7F' locomotives, designed by Henry Fowler, were built for the Somerset and Dorset Joint Railway Company to haul heavy goods and coal trains over the Mendip Hills. Six of the locomotives (numbered 80 to 85) were initially built at the Midland Railway Locomotive Works, Derby in 1914. The Midland Railway Company were joint owners of the SDJR at the time, together with the London and South Western Railway Company.
In 1925, a further five were built by the Robert Stephenson Locomotive Company in Darlington. These additional locomotives (numbered 86 to 90) were built with larger Stephenson design boilers to give them more power. However, they were all later re-fitted with the standard size Fowler design boilers during the 1930s and 1950s.
The locomotives were all withdrawn from service between 1959 and 1964. Numbers 53808 and 53809 have been preserved.

No. 57378. LMS (CR). 0-6-0. 'Class 2F' locomotive. Built in May 1894 by St. Rollox in Glasgow as Caledonian Railway number 257 (later LMS 17378 and BR 57378). Withdrawn from service in September 1962 and scrapped in November 1962. (Photo P.79).

'Class 2F'. LMS (CR 'Jumbo Class') – Additional information.
A total of 244 of these locomotives, designed by Dugald Drummond, were built for the Caledonian Railway Company in Scotland between 1883 and 1897.

A number were fitted with 'stove-pipe' chimneys. They were designed for use as standard goods locomotives and were classified as Caledonian Railway 'Jumbo Class' engines.

These 'Jumbo' locomotives were, numerically, the largest class ever built for the Caledonian Railway. They all became part of the LMS stock after 1923 and a total of 238 entered service with BR in 1948. Although built exclusively as goods engines, over 100 members of the class were subsequently fitted with the Westinghouse braking system to enable them to work passenger train services. Over 100 were still operational into the 1960s until the last one was withdrawn from service in 1964. Sadly, no examples were preserved.

LONDON AND NORTH EASTERN RAILWAY LOCOMOTIVES

No. 60001. *Sir Ronald Matthews*. LNER. 4-6-2. 'Class A4' locomotive. Built at Doncaster in April 1938 as LNER number 4500 (later LNER No.1 & BR 60001). Upon entering service she carried the name *Garganey* (named after a small duck), but was renamed *Sir Ronald Matthews* in March 1939. Sir Ronald Matthews had been the Chairman of the LNER from 1938 until the railways were nationalised in 1948. 60001 was withdrawn from service in October 1964 and scrapped in December 1964. (Photo P.11).

No. 60022. *Mallard*. LNER. 4-6-2. 'Class A4' locomotive. Built at Doncaster in March 1938 as LNER number 4468 (later LNER No.22 & BR 60022). *Mallard* achieved fame shortly after entering service when she attained a world steam speed record of 126mph (203km/h). She was withdrawn from service in April 1963 and preserved as a part of the national collection of steam locomotives on public display at the National Railway Museum in York. (Photo P.90).

No. 60027. *Merlin*. LNER. 4-6-2. 'Class A4' locomotive. Built at Doncaster in March 1937 as LNER number 4486 (later LNER No.27 & BR 60027). Withdrawn from

service in September 1965 and scrapped in December 1965. (Photo P.90).

No. 60034. *Lord Faringdon*. LNER. 4-6-2. 'Class A4' locomotive. Built at Doncaster in July 1938 as LNER number 4903 (later LNER No.34 & BR 60034). After being built, she was allocated the name *Peregrine* (after a Peregrine Falcon 'Duck Hawk' bird of prey) which she carried until March 1948 when she was renamed *Lord Faringdon*. She was withdrawn from service in August 1966 and scrapped in January 1967. (Photo P.89).

Naming of locomotive 60034.
The 'Class A4' locomotive *Lord Faringdon* was named after Alexander Henderson, 1st Baron Faringdon who was born in 1850 and later became a prominent financier in the City of London and a Liberal Unionist Member of Parliament. He was appointed Chairman of the Great Central Railway Company in 1899, where he remained until the company was absorbed into the LNER in 1923. He was then appointed Deputy Chairman of the LNER until his death in 1934.

The naming of locomotives after Lord Faringdon (and his family) was not confined to the LNER 'Class A4' locomotive number 60034. In 1902, GCR, 'Class 11B' (LNER 'Class D9') locomotive number 1014, was given the name *Sir Alexander* after Lord Faringdon, who at the time was Sir Alexander Henderson. The name *Sir Alexander* was removed from the locomotive in 1913 when a new 'Class 11E' express passenger locomotive, number 429, was named after him.

In 1907, a GCR 'Class 8E' (LNER 'Class C5'), number 364, was named *Lady Henderson*, the wife of Sir Alexander. Locomotive 364 was re-named *Lady Faringdon* in 1917, after her husband was raised to the peerage.

In 1913, the GCR introduced ten 'Class 11E' (LNER 'Class D10') locomotives which were named after GCR Company Directors. The first member of the class, number 429, was named

Sir Alexander Henderson. These locomotives were also known as 'Director Class' locomotives.

In 1917, the GCR built six new four cylinder express passenger locomotives, 'Class 9P' (LNER 'Class B3'), inspired by the LNWR 'Claughton Class' locomotives. The first two were named after GCR Company Directors, with the first of the class, locomotive number 1169 (LNER numbers 6169 & 1494), bearing the name *Lord Faringdon*. The remaining locomotives were named after British military leaders of the First World War. An additional five 'Class 9P' locomotives were built in 1920. These 'Class 9P' locomotives were also referred to as the 'Lord Faringdon Class'.

The GCR 'Class 9P' locomotives were extremely fast and powerful locomotives when they were built but were not cost effective as they consumed vast amounts of coal. For this reason, they were never considered to be very successful locomotives. Number 1169 (LNER 6169), *Lord Faringdon*, never saw BR service as she was withdrawn for scrap on 31 December 1947, the eve of nationalisation. Her name was subsequently transferred to 'Class A4' locomotive, number 60034, on 1 March 1948.

Another former GCR locomotive was named *Butler-Henderson* after Eric Brand Butler-Henderson, the youngest son of Lord and Lady Faringdon. Eric was a Director of the GCR from 1918 until 1922 during the time his father was Chairman of the Board. Eric also became a Director of the LNER after the railway groupings of 1923.

One further GCR locomotive with a name connection to Lord Faringdon was GCR 'Class 1A' (LNER 'Class B8') locomotive, number four (LNER numbers 5004 and 1349). She was named *Glenalmond*, which was a Scottish retreat of Lord and Lady Faringdon. A total of eleven GCR 'Class 1A' locomotives were built between 1913 and 1915. 'Class 1A' was also called the 'Glenalmond Class'. Great Central Railway locomotive number four, *Glenalmond*, survived in service until November 1947 when she was withdrawn and later scrapped.

'Class A4' – Additional information. A total of thirty-five 'Class A4' Streamlined Pacific locomotives, designed by Nigel Gresley, were built at Doncaster between 1935 and 1938. They were designed and built as express passenger locomotives to work the East Coast Main Line between London (King's Cross) and Edinburgh via York and Newcastle. They were given the nickname 'Streaks' due to their streamlined appearance and speed.

One member of the class, number 4468, *Mallard*, set a world record for the fastest steam locomotive when she attained a speed of 126mph (203km/h) on 3 July 1938. The record has never been surpassed.

No. 60062. *Minoru*. LNER. 4-6-2. 'Class A3' locomotive. Built at Doncaster in May 1925 as an LNER (GNR design) 'Class A1' locomotive number 2561 (later LNER No.62 & BR 60062). She was rebuilt as a 'Class A3' in June 1944. 60062 was withdrawn from service in December 1964 and scrapped in February 1965. (Photo P.58).

No. 60066. *Merry Hampton*. LNER. 4-6-2. 'Class A3' locomotive was built as a 'Class A1' in July 1924, by the North British Locomotive Company in Glasgow and numbered LNER 9543 (later LNER 2565, LNER No.66 & BR 60066). She was re-classified as an LNER 'Class A10' in 1945 and was rebuilt as a 'Class A3' in 1948. 60066 was withdrawn from service in September 1963 and scrapped in October 1963. (Photo P.10).

No. 60069. *Sceptre*. LNER. 4-6-2. 'Class A3' locomotive was built as a 'Class A1' in September 1924, by the North British Locomotive Company in Glasgow and numbered LNER 2568 (later LNER No.69 & BR 60069). She was rebuilt as a 'Class A3' in May 1942, withdrawn from service in October 1962 and scrapped in May 1963. (Photo P.73).

No. 60084. *Trigo*. LNER. 4-6-2. 'Class A3' locomotive was built at Doncaster in February 1930 as an LNER (GNR design) 'Class A1' and numbered LNER 2595 (later LNER No.84 and BR 60084). She was re-classified as a

'Class A10' locomotive in 1945 and rebuilt as a 'Class A3' in June 1948. 60084 was withdrawn from service in November 1964 and scrapped in January 1965. (Photo P.104).

No. 60103. *Flying Scotsman*. LNER. 4-6-2. 'Class A3' locomotive was built at Doncaster in February 1923 as an LNER (GNR design) 'Class A1' Pacific locomotive number LNER 1472 (later LNER numbers: 4472, 502 and 103). After nationalisation she was numbered BR E103 and finally BR 60103 which she retained for the remainder of her BR service. After being built, she was given the name *Flying Scotsman* after an express passenger train service which operated from Edinburgh to London King's Cross on the East Coast Main Line. The service had been in operation since 1862.

The locomotive *Flying Scotsman* became famous in 1928 when she launched a new non-stop 10am London, King's Cross to Edinburgh Waverley *Flying Scotsman* passenger service. A specially designed tender which incorporated a corridor was coupled to the locomotive to facilitate crew changes during the eight hour non-stop journey. In 1934, the locomotive became even more famous when she became the first ever locomotive to be officially recorded as attaining a speed of 100mph (160.934km/h). In January 1947, *Flying Scotsman* was rebuilt as a 'Class A3' locomotive having been re-classified as a 'Class A10' locomotive between 1945 and 1947.

60103 was withdrawn from service in January 1963 and was subsequently purchased privately by Alan Peglar for restoration and preservation. During the years that followed, *Flying Scotsman* visited the United States, Canada and Australia and went through several changes of ownership until, in 2004, she was purchased for the nation by the National Railway Museum and is now an important part of the national collection. She is the only 'Class A3' locomotive in preservation. (Photos P.31/32).

No. 60112. *St. Simon*. LNER. 4-6-2. 'Class A3' locomotive was built at Doncaster in September 1923 as an LNER (GNR design)

'Class A1' and numbered LNER 4481 (later LNER No.112 & BR 60112). She was re-classified as an LNER 'Class A10' locomotive in 1945 before being rebuilt as a 'Class A3' in August 1946. She was withdrawn from service in December 1964 and scrapped in February 1965. (Photo P.24).

'Class A3' – Additional information. LNER 'Class A3' locomotives were a development of the GNR 'Class A1' locomotives designed by Nigel Gresley. A total of fifty-two (GNR design) 'Class A1' locomotives were built between 1922 and 1935. In 1923, the GNR was absorbed into the LNER and Nigel Gresley was appointed Chief Mechanical Engineer of the newly formed LNER Company.

Gresley quickly developed a new and more powerful locomotive, the LNER 'Class A3', to supersede his 'Class A1' locomotives. Fifty-one of his 'Class A1' locomotives were subsequently rebuilt as 'Class A3' locomotives between 1927 and 1948. In addition, a further twenty-seven brand new 'Class A3' locomotives were built during the same period, taking the grand total of 'Class A3' locomotives to seventy-eight.

The remaining 'Class A1' locomotive, number 4470 (BR 60113) *Great Northern* (the first 'Class A1' to be built), was not rebuilt as a 'Class A3' but was rebuilt by Edward Thompson in 1945, retaining the classification, 'Class A1' (rebuild). Edward Thompson, who designed the rebuild, was the successor to Gresley who died suddenly in 1941 after a short illness

In April 1945, sixteen former GNR 'Class A1' locomotives which had not yet received their rebuilds into 'Class A3' locomotives were re-classified as LNER 'Class A10' locomotives and remained as such until their rebuilds to 'Class A3' were carried out. This was to make way for a new class of A1 locomotives which were being designed and developed by Arthur Peppercorn.

No. 60113. Great Northern. LNER (GNR). 4-6-2. 'Class A1/1' locomotive was built in April 1922 at Doncaster as an LNER (Gresley GNR design) 'Class A1' locomotive number LNER 4470 (later LNER 113 and BR 60113). She was rebuilt by Edward Thompson in September 1945 and remained a 'Class A1' (rebuilt) locomotive. She was the only LNER (GNR) 'Class A1' to be rebuilt by Thompson, as all the other members of the class were rebuilt as Nigel Gresley designed, LNER 'Class A3' locomotives.

In 1947, 60113 was re-classified from a 'Class A1' to a 'Class A1/1' in order to make way for the new 'Class A1' locomotives being built by Arthur Peppercorn which was based on the design of this Thompson rebuild of a Gresley 'Class A1' locomotive. 60113 was withdrawn from service as the sole 'Class A1/1' locomotive in November 1962 and scrapped at Doncaster Works in February 1963. (Photo P.91).

No. 60124. *Kenilworth*. LNER. 4-6-2. Peppercorn 'Class A1' locomotive. Built at Doncaster in March 1949. Withdrawn from service in March 1966 and scrapped in August 1966. (Photo P.59).

No. 60147. *North Eastern*. LNER. 4-6-2. Peppercorn 'Class A1' locomotive. Built at Darlington in April 1949. Withdrawn from service in August 1964 and scrapped in November 1964. Named in March 1952, 60147 was one of four 'Class A1' locomotives named after constituent companies of the LNER. Each of the four locomotives had specially made nameplates with hand-painted coat of arms. (Photo P.18).

'Class A1'. The 1948 Peppercorn design 'Class A1' – Additional information. A total of forty-nine 'Class A1' locomotives, designed by Arthur Peppercorn, were built for British Railways at Doncaster and Darlington between 1948 and 1949. These locomotives should not be confused with the earlier Gresley LNER (GNR) 'Class A1' locomotives built between 1922 & 1935, as they were a completely different design.

The Peppercorn A1 locomotives were however based on a modified version of the Nigel Gresley 'Class A1' design, the modified version being locomotive number 60113, *Great Northern*, after it had been rebuilt by Edward Thompson in 1945.

The Peppercorn 'Class A1' locomotive, was primarily designed as a powerful passenger locomotive to haul the heaviest post war passenger trains in Britain, at the time, on the East Coast Main Line between London and Aberdeen via York and Edinburgh. Some were however later used to haul freight services, a job they were never designed for, and the whole class were given a power classification of 8P6F. All were withdrawn from service between 1962 and 1966. None was preserved.

No. 60504. *Mons Meg*. LNER. 4-6-2. 'Class A2/2' locomotive. Built at Doncaster in July 1936 as LNER number 2004 (later LNER 504 & BR 60504). Withdrawn from service in January 1961 and scrapped in January 1961. (Photo P.11).

No. 60520. *Owen Tudor*. LNER. 4-6-2. 'Class A2/3' locomotive. Built at Doncaster in March 1947 as LNER 520 (later BR 60520). Withdrawn from service in June 1963 and scrapped in August 1963. (Photo P.10).

Serious accident involving 60520 *Owen Tudor*.
On 7 January 1957, *Owen Tudor* was involved in an accident in which one person was killed and twenty-five injured whilst she was hauling the Aberdeen to King's Cross night express. As the train approached Welwyn Garden City, Hertfordshire, at dawn, she over-ran two danger signals and activated warning detonators without reducing speed before running into the back of a local passenger train, wrecking its rear two coaches. 60520, *Owen Tudor*, overturned and her leading six coaches were derailed. The driver suffered severe shock and minor injuries but was discharged from hospital a few days later. Miraculously, the fireman escaped unhurt. The person fatally injured in the accident was a passenger travelling in the rear coach of the local train. 60520 suffered extensive damage but was salvaged from the wreckage and later repaired.

'Class A2' locomotives – Additional information

Class A2/2. Only six 'Class A2/2' locomotives were ever built. Designed by Edward Thompson, they were rebuilds of Gresley's 'Class P2', 2-8-2 express passenger locomotive but were not a huge success. They were all withdrawn from service and scrapped between 1959 and 1961.

Class A2/3. A total of fifteen LNER 'Class A2/3' locomotives designed by Edward Thompson for express passenger work were built in 1946. A further fifteen were due to be built, but following the retirement of Thompson, they were re-designed by his successor Arthur Peppercorn and introduced in 1947 and 1948 as Peppercorn 'Class A2' mixed traffic locomotives (8P7F).

LNER 'Class A2' Pacific locomotives – Sequence of production and designers.

LNER (NER) Raven design 'Class A2' locomotives. Five were built between 1922 and 1925.

LNER Thompson design 'Class A2/1' locomotives (V2 rebuilds). Four were built in 1944.

LNER Thompson design 'Class A2/2' locomotives (P2 rebuilds). Six were built 1943/45.

LNER Thompson design 'Class A2/3' locomotives (new design). Fifteen were built in 1946.

LNER Peppercorn design 'Class A2' locomotives. Fifteen built for BR between 1947 and 1948.

No. 60859. LNER. 2-6-2. 'Class V2' locomotive. Built at Darlington in May 1939 as LNER number 4830 (later LNER 859 & BR 60859). Withdrawn from service in September 1965 and scrapped in October 1965. Fitted with a double chimney in 1961. (Photo P.45).

No. 60867. LNER. 2-6-2. 'Class V2' locomotive. Built at Darlington in July 1939 as LNER number 4838 (later LNER 867 & BR 60867). Withdrawn from service in May 1962 and scrapped in May 1962. (Photo P.74).

No. 60895. LNER. 2-6-2. 'Class V2' locomotive. Built at Darlington in January 1940 as LNER number 4866 (later LNER 895 & BR 60895). Withdrawn from service in October 1965 and scrapped in November 1965. (Photo P.44).

No. 60929. LNER. 2-6-2. 'Class V2' locomotive. Built at Doncaster in June 1941 as LNER number 3656 (later LNER 929 & BR 60929). Withdrawn from service in June 1965 and scrapped in August 1965. (Photo P.75).

No. 60930. LNER. 2-6-2. 'Class V2' locomotive. Built at Doncaster in July 1941 as LNER number 3657 (later LNER 930 & BR 60930). Withdrawn from service in September 1962 and scrapped in November 1962. (Photo P.66).

'Class V2' – Additional information. A total of 184 LNER 'Class V2' locomotives, designed by Nigel Gresley, were built at Darlington and Doncaster between 1936 and 1944. They were designed for use as a mixed traffic locomotive (6MT-later re-classified 7P6F) for hauling express freight trains and passenger services. The first member of the class, number LNER 4771 (BR 60800), was given the name *Green Arrow* (named after an express freight service) and is the only member of the class to have been preserved.

No. 61018. *GNU.* LNER. 4-6-0. 'Class B1' locomotive. Built at Darlington in April 1947 as LNER number 1018 (later BR 61018). Withdrawn from service in November 1965 and scrapped in December 1965. (Photo P.77).

No. 61049. LNER. 4-6-0. 'Class B1' locomotive. Built in June 1946 by the North British Locomotive Company in Glasgow as LNER number 1049 (later BR 61049). Withdrawn from service in November 1965 and scrapped in December 1965. (Photo P.27).

No. 61303. LNER. 4-6-0 'Class B1' locomotive. Built in March 1948 by the North British Locomotive Company in Glasgow as BR number 61303. Withdrawn from service in November 1966 and scrapped in February 1967. (Photo P.103).

No. 61304. LNER. 4-6-0. 'Class B1' locomotive. Built in March 1948 by the North British Locomotive Company in Glasgow as BR number 61304. Withdrawn from service in October 1965 and scrapped in December 1965. (Photo P.56).

No. 61328. LNER. 4-6-0. 'Class B1' locomotive. Built in June 1948 by the North British Locomotive Company in Glasgow as BR number 61328. Withdrawn from service in September 1963 and scrapped in January 1964. (Photo P.78).

No. 61329. LNER. 4-6-0. 'Class B1' locomotive. Built in June 1948 by the North British Locomotive Company in Glasgow as BR number 61329. Withdrawn from service in April 1966 and scrapped in May 1966. (Photo P.103).

'Class B1' – Additional information.
A total of 410 LNER 'Class B1' locomotives, designed by Edward Thompson, were built between 1942 and 1952. These two cylinder locomotives were designed as mixed traffic locomotives to be on a par with the GWR 'Hall Class' and the LMS 'Black 5' locomotives but were of lesser quality due to cost cutting and austerity measures imposed during and after the Second World War. Nevertheless, they were popular locomotives which performed well and proved themselves to be very reliable and efficient mixed traffic locomotives (5MT).

Of the 410 'Class B1' locomotives built, fifty-nine were given names. The first forty members of the class were named after breeds of the South African antelope which gave rise to the whole class being nicknamed 'bongos' or 'antelopes'. A further eighteen were named after LNER Company Directors, many of whom were

unfamiliar names to the public at large. One locomotive, number 61379, was named *Mayflower* after it was built in 1951, to commemorate the Pilgrim Fathers voyage on the ship Mayflower in 1620. Just two members of the class have been preserved.

No. 61420. LNER (NER). 4-6-0. 'Class B16/3' locomotive. Built at Darlington in December 1920 for the North Eastern Railway as NER number 924 (later LNER 924, LNER 1420 & BR 61420). Withdrawn from service in September 1963 and scrapped in February 1964. (Photo P.27).

No. 61436. LNER (NER). 4-6-0. 'Class B16/1' (Raven) locomotive. Built at Darlington in December 1922, entered service as LNER number 2365 (later LNER 1436 & BR 61436). Withdrawn from service in September 1961 and scrapped in March 1962. (Photo P.102).

'Class B16' (former NER 'Class S3') – Additional information.
A total of seventy NER 'Class S3' locomotives, designed by Vincent Raven, were built by the North Eastern Railway Company between 1919 and 1924. They were three-cylinder mixed traffic locomotives, with a power classification of 6MT - later re-classified 5MT by BR. The locomotives were absorbed into the stock of the LNER when the railway groupings took place in 1923 and they were re-classified as LNER 'Class B16' locomotives.

The LNER later decided to rebuild some of the class. The original Vincent Raven design (un-rebuilt) engines were all re-classified as 'Class B16/1' locomotives.

Seven locomotives which were rebuilt by Nigel Gresley between 1937 and 1940 were classified as 'Class B16/2' locomotives.

A further seventeen members of the class, rebuilt by Edward Thompson between 1942 and 1949 were classified as 'Class B16/3' locomotives.

No. 61756. LNER (GNR). 2-6-0. 'Class K2/2' locomotive. Originally built in July 1918 by the North British Locomotive

Works in Glasgow as a GNR 'Class H3' locomotive number 4666 (later LNER 1756 & BR 61756). She was re-classified as a 'Class K2' by the LNER after 1923 and later she was further re-classified as a 'K2/2'. She was withdrawn from service in June 1962 and later scrapped. (Photo P.100).

'Class K1 and K2' (Gresley). (Former GNR 'Class H2' & 'Class H3') – Additional information.
A total of ten GNR 'Class H2' locomotives were designed and built by Nigel Gresley in 1912. They were designed as mixed traffic locomotives but were under-powered and only moderately successful. In 1923 they were re-classified as LNER 'Class K1' locomotives.

Gresley then made a number of modifications to the design between 1914 and 1921, before introducing sixty-five new GNR 'Class H3' locomotives which were later re-classified as LNER 'Class K2' locomotives. These new locomotives had larger boilers and were a complete success.

The first batch of ten GNR 'Class H2' locomotives (LNER 'Class K1') were rebuilt to the same design as the new engines and classified as LNER 'Class K2/1' locomotives. The sixty-five 'Class K2' locomotives were then re-classified as 'Class K2/2' locomotives.

No. 61814. LNER (GNR). 2-6-0. 'Class K3/2' locomotive. Built at Darlington in September 1924 as LNER number 36 (later LNER 1814 & BR 61814). Withdrawn from service in December 1961 and scrapped in January 1962. (Photo P.51).

No. 61935. LNER. 2-6-0. 'Class K3/2' locomotive. Built by Robert Stephenson & Hawthorn Ltd, Darlington in December 1934 as LNER number 1322 (later LNER 1935 & BR 61935). Withdrawn from service in July 1962 and scrapped in July 1962. (Photo P.101).

'Class K3' (former GNR 'Class H4') – Additional information.
In 1920, Nigel Gresley introduced ten 'Class H4' locomotives onto the GNR. They

were powerful mixed traffic locomotives with six-foot diameter boilers, the largest boilers ever seen on British locomotives at that time. After the 1923 railway groupings took place, the ten locomotives were absorbed into the LNER as LNER 'Class K3' locomotives and a further 183 were built between 1923 and 1937. These locomotives were classified simply as 'Class K3' until 1947 when the class was divided as follows.

The original ten locomotives built for the GNR were re-classified as 'Class K3/1'. The engines built by the LNER were re-classified as 'Class K3/2' and a batch of locomotives fitted with the Westinghouse braking system were classified as 'Class K3/3'. Some other locomotives which had received other modifications were classified as 'Classes K3/4, K3/5 & K3/6'. One other member of the class, locomotive number LNER 1863 (BR 61863), was rebuilt as a 'Class K5' locomotive by Edward Thompson in 1945. Some 'Class K3' locomotives were fitted with GNR tenders.

No. 62059. LNER. 2-6-0. 'Class K1' locomotive. Built in December 1949 by the North British Locomotive Company, Glasgow as BR number 62059. Withdrawn from service in February 1967 and scrapped in June 1967. (Photo P.57).

'Class K1' (Thompson). - Additional information.
A total of seventy 'Class K1' locomotives designed by Edward Thompson were built by the North British Locomotive Company in Glasgow between 1949 and 1950. These engines were simple two-cylinder locomotives as opposed to the three-cylinder designs preferred by Gresley. They were designed and built as mixed traffic locomotives (5P6F) and were the last steam locomotives of LNER design ever built for BR. One member of the class, number 62005, has been preserved.

No. 63920. LNER. 2-8-0, 'Class 04/6' locomotive. Built at Gorton Locomotive Works (Gorton Tank), Manchester in

February 1924 as LNER 3920 (later BR 63920). Withdrawn from service in August 1962 and scrapped in November 1962. (Photo P.38).

LNER 'Class 04' (Former GCR 'Class 8K') – Additional information.
A total of 126 GCR 'Class 8K' 2-8-0 heavy freight locomotives, designed by John Robinson, were built between 1911 and the outbreak of the First World War in 1914. The locomotive building programme for the GCR 'Class 04' was suspended during the war years but continued after the war in 1918.

During the actual war years, a further 500 of these 2-8-0 locomotives were built for the British government to be used by the Railway Operating Division of the British Army (Royal Engineers), for wartime requirements home and abroad.

In 1923, the LNER inherited 131 'Class 8K' locomotives from the GCR and re-classified them as LNER 'Class 04'. The LNER later purchased 273 similar locomotives from the ROD which had been built for wartime use. These were also classified as LNER 'Class 04' locomotives.

LNER 'Class 04' – The locomotives were sub-divided as follows:
'Class 04/1' = Original GCR 'Class 8K' engines built between 1911 and 1914.

'Class 04/2' = ROD engines with reduced cab & boiler height for loading gauge.

'Class 04/3' = ROD engines with steam brake only (no vacuum brake) and no water scoop. 'Class 04/2' and 'Class 04/3' locomotives were all re-classified as 'Class 04/1' in 1947.

'Class 04/4' = Used for 'Class 8K' engines which were rebuilt with '02 boilers'.

'Class 04/5' = Engines rebuilt after 1932 with boiler and firebox modifications.

'Class 04/6' = Originally LNER 'Class 05' locomotives rebuilt with smaller boilers.

'Class 04/7' = Engines rebuilt after 1939 with similar modification to the 'Class 04/5'.

'Class 04/8' = Engines rebuilt after 1944 with 'Class B1' type boilers and side-window cab.

No. 63946. LNER. 2-8-0. 'Class 02/2' locomotive. Built at Doncaster in June 1924 as LNER number 3946 (later BR 63946). Withdrawn from service on 7 April 1963 and scrapped in September 1963. (Photo P.39).

No. 63973. LNER. 2-8-0. 'Class 02/3' locomotive. Built at Doncaster in October 1942 as LNER number 3973 (later BR 63973). Withdrawn from service in September 1963 and scrapped in February 1964. (Photo P.52).

'Class 02' – Additional information.
The first Gresley design 'Class 02', three-cylinder locomotive was built for the GNR in 1918. A further sixty-six were built between 1921 and 1943 in various batches with a number of modifications to each batch. A number were later rebuilt. All GNR locomotives were absorbed into the LNER in January 1923 and the 'Class 02' locomotives were later divided into sub-classes as follows.

The first member of the class (63921) built in 1918 remained a 'Class 02'. This locomotive differed from the rest of the class by having inclined cylinders as opposed to horizontal cylinders. The first batch of ten locomotives, introduced in 1921, became 'Class 02/1' (some were later rebuilt). The next batch of fifteen locomotives were introduced in 1924 after the GNR had been absorbed into the LNER. They were classified as 'Class 02/2'. In 1932, sixteen 'Class 02/3' locomotives were introduced (development of the 02/2). From 1943 onwards, twenty-five 'Class 02/2' and 'Class 02/3' were rebuilt by Edward Thompson as 'Class 02/4' locomotives.

The 'Class 02' locomotives were very successful heavy freight locomotives and ideal for hauling long and heavy iron-ore, coal and ballast trains.

No. 64277. LNER (GNR). 0-6-0. 'Class J6' locomotive. Built at Doncaster in August 1922 as GNR number 638 (later LNER 3638 and 4277 & BR 64277). Withdrawn from service in June 1962 and scrapped in June 1962. (Photo P.24).

'Class J6' (GNR 'Classes 521 & 536') – Additional information.
A total of 110 GNR 0-6-0 'Class 536' locomotives designed by Henry Ivatt and Nigel Gresley were built between 1911 and 1922. The first fifteen were built to the design of Ivatt ('Class 521') and the remainder were slightly modified by Gresley ('Class 536').

They were designed primarily as light goods locomotives (power classification 3F) but were soon found to be very versatile engines and were frequently used to work passenger train services. As such, they became used for general mixed-traffic duties.

All 110 locomotives passed to British Railways in 1948 and were withdrawn from service between 1955 and 1962.

No. 65224. *Mons.* LNER (NBR). 0-6-0. 'Class J36' locomotive. Built at the Cowlairs Locomotive Works, Glasgow in February 1891 for the North British Railway Company as NBR number 648 (later LNER 9648, 5224 and BR 65224).

65224 was shipped to France for service during the First World War and upon return to the UK she was given the name *Mons*, after the 1914 battle which took place in and around the Belgian town of Mons which is situated near the French/Belgian border.

Number 65224 was withdrawn from service in May 1963 and scrapped in March 1964. (Photo P.44).

No. 65345. LNER (NBR). 0-6-0. 'Class J36' locomotive. Built at the Cowlairs Locomotive Works, Glasgow in December 1900 for the North British Railway Company as NBR number 793 (later LNER 9793, 5345 and BR 65345). Withdrawn from service in June 1967 and scrapped in November 1967. This locomotive was also used as a stationary boiler at Thornton Junction Shed (Shed number 62A). (Photo No.43).

'Class J36' (NBR 'Class C') – Additional Information.
A total of 168 of these locomotives were built for the North British Railway between 1888 and 1901. They were designed by Matthew Holmes as general goods locomotives (power classification BR 2F). Twenty-five of these engines were shipped to France during the First World War under the control of the Railway Operating Division of the British Army, Royal Engineers. Upon returning to Britain, they were each given names of British Generals and Battles appertaining to the conflict.

123 of these engines survived until after 1948 and saw BR service. The last three members of the class were withdrawn from service in 1966.

No. 65844. LNER (NER). 0-6-0. 'Class J27' locomotive. Built by Beyer, Peacock Ltd in August 1908 as NER number 1211 (later LNER 5844 & BR 65844). Withdrawn from service in December 1965 and scrapped in May 1966. (Photo P.102).

No. 65894. LNER (NER). 0-6-0. 'Class J27' locomotive. Built at Darlington in September 1923 as LNER number 2392 (later LNER 5894 and BR 65894). Withdrawn from service in September 1967 and was purchased privately from BR by the North Eastern Railway Preservation Group, for restoration and preservation. 65894 is currently based at the Darlington Railway Museum. The locomotive is fully operational and is frequently hired for use on private heritage railways. It has worked in England, Scotland and Wales on the North Yorkshire Moors Railway, Bo'ness & Kinneil Railway, Llangollen Railway, Keighley & Worth Valley Railway, North Norfolk Railway, East Lancashire Railway and several other private railways and should continue to do so for many years. (Photo P.102).

'Class J27' (former NER 'Class 3P') – Additional information.
A total of 115 LNER (NER) 'Class J27' were built between 1906 and 1922. The first eighty were built between 1906 and 1909 in five batches. The remainder were built over a decade later between 1921 and 1923.

The locomotives were originally designed for the North Eastern Railway Company by Wilson Worsdell as 'Class P3' goods locomotives, based upon the design of the earlier NER 'Class P2' engines but with some modifications, including a larger firebox. 'Class P3' locomotives were later re-classified as 'Class J27' locomotives by the LNER in 1926. These powerful locomotives were frequently used for working heavy mineral trains and were a common site on the Durham coalfields. They were also well suited for working long goods trains and could often be seen hauling goods traffic between York and the north-east holiday resort town of Scarborough. Originally given a power classification 4F, they were re-classified as 5F in 1953.

No. 65923. LNER. 0-6-0. 'Class J38' locomotive. Built at Darlington in March 1926 as LNER number 1427 (later LNER 5923 & BR 65923). Withdrawn from service in December 1962 and scrapped in January 1963. (Photo P.65).

'Class J38' – Additional information.
Thirty-five 0-6-0 'Class J38' freight locomotives (6F), designed by Nigel Gresley, were built for the LNER in 1926, for use in Scotland. They all passed into BR ownership in 1949. Gresley later introduced a total of 289 almost identical locomotives for general use on the LNER. They were the 'Class J39' locomotives, with larger driving wheels than the 'Class J38'. These powerful, versatile locomotives were successfully used as mixed traffic locomotives.

All the 'Class J38' locomotives were scrapped between 1962 and 1967.

No. 67759. LNER. 2-6-4T. 'Class L1' locomotive. Built by the North British

Locomotive Company, Glasgow in December 1948. Withdrawn from service in October 1962 and scrapped in March 1963. (Photo P.35).

'Class L1' – Additional information.
A single prototype 'Class L1' Tank locomotive, designed by Edward Thompson, was built for the LNER in 1945. A further ninety-nine were later built by BR between 1948 and 1950.

These 2-6-4 tank locomotives were designed for use as suburban passenger locomotives and whilst their 5ft 2in driving wheels gave them excellent power at low speed, they were not well suited running at the higher speeds required for passenger work. It soon became apparent that these locomotives were better suited to freight duties and were accordingly afforded a mixed traffic status, with a power classification of BR 4MT. They were all withdrawn from service between 1960 and 1962 and later scrapped.

No. 68726. LNER (NER). 0-6-0T. 'Class J72' Tank locomotive. Built by Armstrong Whitworth at Newcastle in April 1922 as NER number 2319 (later LNER 8726 & BR 68726). Withdrawn from service in June 1961 and scrapped in June 1961. (Photo P.109).

No. 68736. LNER (NER). 0-6-0T. 'Class J72' Tank locomotive. Built in June 1922 by Armstrong Whitworth, Newcastle as NER number 2359 (later LNER 8736 & BR 68736). Withdrawn from service in October 1963 and scrapped in December 1963. (Photo P.11).

Two 'Class J72' locomotives, numbers 68736 (above) and 68723, were selected to perform 'pilot duties' at York and Newcastle railway stations in the 1950s. As a result, both engines were re-painted in North Eastern Railway light green livery, whilst retaining their BR numbers. Although the photographs in this book are black and white, the photograph taken of number 68736 at York Station in 1960, alongside 'Class A4' locomotive number 60001 *Sir Ronald Matthews*, shows her turned out in NER green livery.

'Class J72' Tank (former NER 'Class E1') – Additional information.
A total of 113 'Class J72' Tank locomotives were built for the NER, LNER & BR over a staggering 53 year period from 1898 to 1951. These small tank locomotives (power classification 2F), were originally designed by Wilson Worsdell for the NER as 'Class E1' shunting engines. They were re-classified as LNER 'Class J72' tank locomotives after 1923.

Twenty were initially built between 1898 and 1899 by Worsdell for the NER. A further twenty were built fifteen years later by Vincent Raven in 1914 and an additional thirty-five were built for the NER between 1920 and 1922. Nigel Gresley then built a further ten for the LNER in 1925, taking the total build to eighty-five.

Surprisingly, Arthur Peppercorn ordered a further twenty-eight 'Class J72' locomotives for BR service. They were built between 1949 and 1951 and were still very similar in design to those built by Worsdell for the NER in 1898. The last locomotives in the class continued working on the BR network until they were withdrawn from service in 1963. They were amazing little engines.

No. 68934. LNER 'Class J50/2' Tank locomotive. Built at Doncaster in March 1924 as LNER number 3235 (later LNER 8934 & BR 68934). Withdrawn from service in September 1963 and scrapped in November 1963. (Photo P.35).

'Class J50' Tank – (Former GNR 'Class J23') – Additional information.
A total of 102 GNR 'Class J23' Tank locomotives, designed by Nigel Gresley, were built between 1913 and 1939. These 0-6-0 tank locomotives were primarily built to work local coal trains and for use as shunting engines. They had a power classification BR 4F. Due to their long side-tanks they were given the nickname 'submarines'.

The GNR 'Class J23' locomotives were introduced in various batches with modifications in each batch which included the use of two different size boilers. After the GNR locomotives were absorbed into LNER stock in 1923, they were re-classified from 'Class J23' as follows; Locomotives fitted with the larger boilers became LNER 'Class J50' and the ones with the smaller boilers became LNER 'Class J51'.

'Class J50' locomotives were further sub-divided into J50/1 and J50/2 and the 'Class J51' locomotives were sub-divided into J51/1, J51/2, J51/3 and J51/4. These sub-divisions were determined by the various modifications which the locomotives had received during their twenty-six years construction period.

BRITISH RAILWAYS LOCOMOTIVES

No. 70002. *Geoffrey Chaucer*. BR. 4-6-2. 'Britannia Class' locomotive. Built at Crewe in March 1951 as a mixed traffic locomotive (7P6F). Withdrawn from service in January 1967 and scrapped in May 1967. (Photo P.61).

No. 70013. *Oliver Cromwell*. BR. 4-6-2. 'Britannia Class' locomotive. Built at Crewe in May 1951. Withdrawn from service in August 1968 and preserved as a part of the national collection at the National Railway Museum in York. (Photo P.60).

No. 70015. *Apollo*. BR. 4-6-2. 'Britannia Class' locomotive. Built at Crewe in June 1951. Withdrawn from service in August 1967 and scrapped in January 1968. (Photos P.18 and P.84).

No. 70022. *Tornado*. BR. 4-6-2. 'Britannia Class' locomotive. Built at Crewe in August 1951. Withdrawn from service in December 1967 and scrapped in March 1968. (Photo P.72).

No. 70049. *Solway Firth*. BR. 4-6-2. 'Britannia Class' locomotive. Built at Crewe in July 1954. Withdrawn from service in December 1967 and scrapped in March 1968. (Photo P.61).

'Britannia Class' (BR Standard Class 7) – Additional information.
A total of fifty-five BR 'Standard Class 7' (Britannia Class), 'Pacific' locomotives,

designed by Robert Riddles for mixed traffic duties (7P6F), were built at Crewe between 1951 and 1954. Some mechanical problems emerged shortly after these locomotives entered service, which resulted in twenty-five members of the class being withdrawn for modifications. Locomotive crews had mixed opinions about the engines but they were well received on the Eastern Region of BR where they were generally considered as good, versatile locomotives. Just two members of the class have been preserved, number 70000, *Britannia,* and number 70013, *Oliver Cromwell.*

No. 72000. *Clan Buchanan*. BR. 4-6-2. 'Clan Class' locomotive. Built at Crewe in December 1951. Withdrawn from service in December 1962 and scrapped in September 1963. (Photo P.19).

No. 72008. *Clan MacLeod*. BR. 4-6-2. 'Clan Class' locomotive. Built at Crewe in March 1952. Withdrawn from service in April 1966 and scrapped in June 1966. (Photo P.62).

No. 72009. *Clan Stewart*. BR. 4-6-2. 'Clan Class' locomotive. Built at Crewe in March 1952. Withdrawn from service in August 1965 and scrapped in November 1965. (Photo P.98).

'Clan Class' (BR Standard Class 6) – Additional information.
A total of ten BR 'Standard Class 6' (Clan Class), 'Pacific' locomotives, designed by Robert Riddles, were built at Crewe between 1951 and 1952. They were in effect a smaller and lighter version of his 'Britannia Class' design to increase route availability where Britannia locomotives were prohibited from operating due to weight restrictions. Unfortunately, because of their lesser power classification (6P5F), crews often complained of lack of pulling power which was exacerbated by the single chimney design. Crews who were unfamiliar with the locomotives often found them difficult to handle.
Due to the small number of 'Clan Class' locomotives built, they were mainly confined to sheds in Glasgow and Carlisle.

Initially it was proposed that twenty-five 'Clan Class' locomotives would be built but after the first ten were introduced, the plans for another fifteen were put on hold and eventually abandoned.

No. 73015. BR. 4-6-0. 'Standard Class 5' locomotive. Built at Derby in September 1951. Withdrawn from service in August 1965 and scrapped in November 1965. (Photo P.67).

No. 73018. BR. 4-6-0. 'Standard Class 5' locomotive. Built at Derby in September 1951. Withdrawn from service in July 1967 and scrapped in January 1968. (Photo P.81).

No. 73043. BR. 4-6-0. 'Standard Class 5' locomotive. Built at Derby in October 1953. Withdrawn from service in July 1967 and scrapped in March 1968. (Photo P.82).

No. 73046. BR. 4-6-0. 'Standard Class 5' locomotive. Built at Derby in November 1953. Withdrawn from service in September 1964 and scrapped in March 1965. (Photo P.85).

No. 73062. BR. 4-6-0. 'Standard Class 5' locomotive. Built at Derby in October 1954. Withdrawn from service in June 1965 and scrapped in November 1965. (Photo P.68).

No. 73068. BR. 4-6-0. 'Standard Class 5' locomotive. Built at Derby in October 1954. Withdrawn from service in December 1965 and scrapped in April 1966. Some of the Standard Five locomotives on the Western Region were painted green as opposed to black. This locomotive, based at Bristol, Barrow Road Shed (Shed number 82E) (post 1958) was one such example. (Photo P.88).

***No. 73085**. *Melisande*. BR. 4-6-0. 'Standard Class 5' locomotive. Built at Derby in August 1955. Withdrawn from service in July 1967 and scrapped in April 1968. (Photo P.48).

***No. 73086**. *The Green Knight*. BR. 4-6-0. 'Standard Class 5' locomotive. Built at Derby in August 1955. Withdrawn from service in October 1966 and scrapped in March 1967. (Photo P.49).

No. **73171**. BR. 4-6-0. 'Standard Class 5' locomotive. Built at Doncaster in May 1957. Withdrawn from service in October 1966 and scrapped in March 1967. (Photo P.84).

Naming of 'BR Standard Class 5' locomotives.
Initially, 'Standard Class 5' locomotives were not given names. However, in 1959, a total of twenty locomotives (numbers 73080 to 73119 inclusive) were allocated names of former SR (LSWR) 'Class N15' 'King Arthur Class' locomotives which were being withdrawn from service. Locomotive numbers 73085 & 73086, both listed above (marked *), bear names transferred from 'King Arthur Class' locomotives and are pictured in this book.

'Standard Class 5' – Additional information.
A total of 172 BR Standard 'Class 5' locomotives were built between 1951 and 1957. These 4-6-0 mixed traffic locomotives (5MT), designed by Robert Riddles, were a development of the very successful LMS 'Class Five' (Black Five) locomotive but were more economical and easier to maintain. They were quite capable of hauling 100 MPH express passenger trains whilst using poor quality coal.

No. **75006**. BR. 4-6-0. 'Standard Class 4/1' locomotive. Built at Swindon in September 1951. Withdrawn from service in August 1967 and scrapped in February 1968. (Photo P.89).

No. **75007**. BR. 4-6-0. 'Standard Class 4/1' locomotive. Built at Swindon in September 1951. Withdrawn from service in March 1965 and scrapped in August 1965. (Photo P.67).

No. **75051**. BR. 4-6-0. 'Standard Class 4/1' locomotive. Built at Swindon in November 1956. Withdrawn from service in October 1966 and scrapped in February 1967. (Photo P.88).

'Standard Class 4' locomotives (Designed by Robert Riddles) – Additional information.

There were three types of 'Standard Class 4' locomotives as follows:

'Class 4/1' = 4-6-0. Tender locomotives (4MT) built between 1951 & 1957. (Total eighty.)

'Class 4/2' = 2-6-0. Tender locomotives (4MT) built between 1952 & 1957. (Total 115.)

'Class 4/3' = 2-6-4. Tank locomotives (4MT) built between 1951 & 1957. (Total 155.)

'Standard Class 4/1'
A total of eighty, 'Standard Class 4/1', 4-6-0 tender locomotives were built between 1951 and 1957 as mixed traffic locomotives (4MT) for use on secondary routes where 'Class 5' locomotives were unable to operate due to locomotive weight restrictions. They were in effect a tender version of the 'Standard Class 4' 2-6-4 Tank engine. They were all withdrawn from service between 1964 and 1968. Six were subsequently preserved.

'Standard Class 4/2'
A total of 115 'Standard Class 4/2', 2-6-0 tender locomotives were built between 1952 and 1957. They were based upon the design of the LMS, Ivatt 'Class 4' locomotive, of which 162 were produced between 1947 and 1952. They were intended to be used as freight locomotives (LMS classification 4F) but were frequently used to work secondary passenger services and as a result, were later re-classified by BR as 4MT locomotives.

'Standard Class 4/3'
A total of 155 'Standard Class 4/3', 2-6-4 Tank locomotives were built between 1951 and 1957. They were based upon the design of the LMS Fairburn, 2-6-4 tank locomotive but with a number of modifications. A total of 277 Fairburn design locomotives had been built between 1945 and 1951 for working secondary passenger trains (LMS Class 4P).

The BR 'Standard Class 4/3' was built for mixed traffic duties (4MT) but it was soon realised that they were particularly suited for working commuter traffic and they became a familiar site on the Liverpool Street to Southend and Tilbury lines. They were also extensively used on the London to Brighton line and for working commuter services from London to East Sussex and Kent. In addition, they were used on commuter services in Glasgow.

No. 78022. BR. 2-6-0. 'Standard Class 2/1' locomotive. Built at Darlington in May 1954. Withdrawn from service in September 1966 and subsequently preserved by the Standard 4 Locomotive Society. Currently working on the Keighley & Worth Valley Heritage Railway. (Photo P.87).

'Standard Class 2' locomotives (Designed by Robert Riddles). – Additional information. There were two types of 'Standard Class 2' locomotives as follows;

'Class 2/1' = 2-6-0. Tender locomotives (4MT). A total of sixty-five were built between 1952 and 1956. This locomotive design was based on the LMS Ivatt 'Class 2', 2-6-0 locomotive and was the smallest of all the BR Standard locomotive designs. Not surprisingly they were given the nickname, 'Mickey Mouse'.

'Class 2/2' = 2-6-2. Tank locomotives (4MT). A total of thirty were built between 1953 and 1957. This locomotive design was based on the LMS Ivatt 'Class 2' 2-6-2 Tank engine, with some modifications, including a smaller cab to reduce the loading gauge height.

Although both types of 'Standard Class 2' locomotives were classified as mixed traffic locomotives, they were built primarily for working light passenger trains and the 'Class 2/2' tank engines were additionally equipped for the push and pull working of passenger trains.

No. 80036. BR. 2-6-4T. 'Standard Class 4/3' Tank locomotive. Built at Brighton in May 1952. Withdrawn from service in November 1964. Scrapped in March 1965. (Photo P.22).

No. 80050. BR. 2-6-4T. 'Standard Class 4/3' Tank locomotive. Built at Brighton in November 1952. Withdrawn from service in November 1964 and scrapped in July 1965. (Photo P.72).

No. 90047. BR (WD). 2-8-0. 'Class WD' Austerity locomotive. Built in April 1944 by the North British Locomotive Company in Glasgow for the Government War Department (WD) as WD number 63047 (later BR 90047). Withdrawn from service in June 1967 and scrapped in February 1968. (Photo P.97).

No. 90339. BR (WD). 2-8-0. 'Class WD' (Austerity) locomotive. Built in August 1944 by the North British Locomotive Company in Glasgow. Withdrawn from service in July 1967 and scrapped in October 1967. (Photo P.66).

No. 90488. BR (WD). 2-8-0. 'Class WD' (Austerity) locomotive. Built in July 1944 by the Vulcan Foundry at Newton-le-Willows in Lancashire. Withdrawn from service in December 1964 and scrapped in May 1965. (Photos P.48 and P.99).

No. 90540. BR (WD). 2-8-0. 'Class WD' (Austerity) locomotive. Built in July 1943 by the Vulcan Foundry at Newton-le-Willows in Lancashire. Withdrawn from service in July 1965 and scrapped in April 1966. (Photo P.98).

No. 90610. BR (WD). 2-8-0. 'Class WD' (Austerity) locomotive. Built in January 1944 by the Vulcan Foundry at Newton-le-Willows in Lancashire. Withdrawn from service in May 1967 and scrapped in September 1967. (Photo P.47).

No. 90633. BR (WD). 2-8-0. 'Class WD' (Austerity) locomotive. Built in April 1944 by the Vulcan Foundry at Newton-le-Willows in Lancashire. Withdrawn from service in July 1967 and scrapped in January 1968. (Photo P.103).

'WD Class'. War Department (WD) locomotives – Additional information. A total of 935 'Class WD' (Austerity) locomotives were built by the North British Locomotive Company, Glasgow and the Vulcan Foundry in Lancashire between 1943 and 1945.

These 2-8-0 heavy freight locomotives (8F) were designed by Robert Riddles for use during the Second World War. A number were shipped to various countries abroad for use in the conflict and others were loaned to the 'Big Four' railway companies. The locomotive design was based upon the LMS 2-8-0 'Class 8F' but of lesser quality due to a number of cost cutting modifications which were put in place, in line with the wartime austerity measures.

A larger 2-10-0 version of the 'WD Class' was also introduced during the same period. A total of 150 of the 2-10-0s were built with the same power classification (8F) as the 2-8-0 version but the extra set of wheels and wider firebox spread the axle load, enabling the locomotives to operate on additional lines where weight restrictions were in place which prohibited the 8F locomotives from working.

After the war, the 'Big Four' railway companies purchased the 'WD Class' locomotives which they already had on loan from the War Department. The LNER purchased 200 'WD Class' locomotives in 1946 (including 190 which they already had on loan), and immediately re-classified them as LNER 'Class 07' locomotives. A further 533 were loaned by the WD to BR when the company was formed in January 1948. The British Transport Commission (governing body of BR) purchased the locomotives for BR at the end of that year. All 200 LNER 'Class 07' locomotives were absorbed into BR stock as 'WD Class' locomotives in 1948, together with 'WD Class' locomotives from the remaining three of the 'Big Four' companies. In 1949, all the 'WD Class' locomotives were re-numbered into one series by BR. The only 'WD Class' locomotive to be named in BR service was number 90732. She was named *Vulcan* in recognition of the 'Vulcan Foundry', who assisted in the design and development of the locomotives and built many of them.

Standard Class 9F
No. 92026. BR. 2-10-0. Standard 'Class 9F' locomotive built at Crewe in June 1955. Withdrawn from service in November 1967 and scrapped in April 1968. (Photo P.55).

No. 92138. BR. 2-10-0. Standard 'Class 9F' locomotive. Built at Crewe in July 1957. Withdrawn from service in July 1967. Scrapped in December 1967. (Photo P.36).

No. 92145. BR. 2-10-0. Standard 'Class 9F' locomotive. Built at Crewe in August 1957. Withdrawn from service in February 1966 and scrapped in April 1966. (Photo P.76).

No. 92203. BR. 2-10-0. Standard 'Class 9F' locomotive. Built at Swindon in April 1959. Withdrawn from service in November 1967 and subsequently preserved. 92203 was later given the name *Black Prince* during preservation. She is currently owned by the North Norfolk Heritage Railway where she is based. She is fully operational. (Photo P.36).

No. 92220. *Evening Star*. BR. 2-10-0. Standard 'Class 9F' locomotive. Built at Swindon in March 1960. Withdrawn from service in March 1965 and subsequently preserved. 92220 *Evening Star* is now a part of the 'National Collection' of preserved steam locomotives on public display in the Main Hall of the National Railway Museum in York. (Photo P.109).

No. 92239. BR. 2-10-0. Standard 'Class 9F' locomotive. Built at Crewe in September 1958. Withdrawn from service in November 1966 and scrapped in April 1967. (Photo P.37).

No. 92243. BR. 2-10-0. Standard 'Class 9F' locomotive. Built at Crewe in October 1958. Withdrawn from service in December 1965 and scrapped in April 1966. (Photo P.75).

Standard 'Class 9F' 2-10-0 locomotives – Additional information.
A total of 251 BR Standard 'Class 9F' locomotives, designed by Robert Riddles, were built at Crewe and Swindon between 1954 and 1960. Designed to haul heavy mineral trains, these locomotives were a development of the 'WD Class' 2-10-0 Austerity locomotives. They were the last of the twelve 'BR Standard' classes of locomotive to be built and deemed to be the most successful. They were on occasions called upon to haul passenger trains.

The 'Class 9F' locomotives were all painted in black un-lined livery with a BR crest on each side of the tender. There was, however, one exception. Number 92220 was the last member of the class to be built. She was also the last steam locomotive ever built for BR when she left Swindon Works in March 1960. To mark her special status, she was turned out painted in Brunswick Green livery and fitted with a copper capped chimney. She was allocated the name *Evening Star*, the only member of her class to carry a name during BR service. 92220, *Evening Star,* was earmarked for preservation from the time she was built and she was withdrawn from service after just five years in March 1965. This famous locomotive is now a part of the National Collection of preserved steam locomotives and is on public display at the National Railway Museum in York. A photograph of *Evening Star* is featured in this book.